west coast

cederberg to sea

west coast

landscape • people • food • texture

Karena du Plessis
Vanessa Cowling

First published in 2006 by Struik Publishers
(a division of New Holland Publishing (South Africa) (Pty) Ltd)

New Holland Publishing is a member of Johnnic Commmunications Ltd

Garfield House
86–88 Edgware Road
W2 2EA London
United Kingdom
www.newhollandpublishers.com

Cornelis Struik House
80 McKenzie Street
Cape Town 8001
South Africa
www.struik.co.za

14 Aquatic Drive
Frenchs Forest
NSW 2086
Australia

218 Lake Road
Northcote
Auckland
New Zealand

ISBN 1 77007 188 1 (9 781770 071889)

1 3 5 7 9 10 8 6 4 2

Publishing manager: Dominique le Roux
Managing editor: Lesley Hay-Whitton
Project co-ordinator: Samantha Menezes-Fick
Designer: Martin Jones, Hirt & Carter Cape
Editor: Elizabeth Wilson
Proofreader: Roxanne Reid
Indexer: Ethné Clarke

Reproduction by Hirt & Carter Cape (Pty) Ltd
Printed and bound by Kyodo Printing Co (S'pore) Pte Ltd, Singapore

Permissions

Tannie Evita *(page 48)* This piece by Karena du Plessis first appeared in *Fodor's Southern Africa*, Random House, 2005

Giants of the deep *(page 62)* A version of this article was first published in *The Cape Odyssey*, Volume 3, Issue 5

(page 107) The poem 'O Wittewater' is published with the kind permission of Joyce Johannes

(page 140) 'Waterblommetjies' Words and Music by Anton Goosen © 1978 – AG Music – Administered by Gallo Music Publishers

(pages 41 and 187) Every attempt was made to trace the benefactors of Lawrence Green's estate; extracts from his books are used in good faith.

Front cover: *Early morning in Paternoster, before the fishermen have gone out.* ***Back cover:*** *Pink paper flowers bloom in winter.* ***Page 1:*** *The West Coast is famous for its spectacular shows of spring flowers.* ***Pages 2–3:*** *Langebaan Lagoon at sunset is a symphony of colour, with pink flamingos mirrored in the still water.*

Acknowledgements

There isn't anybody that I met who isn't madly passionate about the West Coast – or their small corner of it. Thanks to all the people at the local tourism bureaux and museums who were so helpful and recommended what I should and shouldn't do and whom I should speak to. There are more than a number of individuals who went out of their way to accommodate me or spend time with me, sharing their knowledge of the area. Thank you for your warmth, humour and unfailing enthusiasm. I also think you live in a unique part of the country with many quiet treasures. Thanks too, to Vanessa Cowling, 'the paparazzi of *bokkoms*', and Alex Bassios who was always happy to drive to strange places and especially keen if the roads were muddy and hazardous!

Karena du Plessis

The people that I have met during this project have changed my life. They have shown me what it is to be truly kind, warm and generous and for that I am deeply thankful! To the people who opened up their homes, kitchens, cellars and hearts, thank you.

I would especially like to thank Julian Melck – for his passionate involvement, for being such a wonderful host and for insisting that I see the landscape from the air. We could not have done this without the help of Mr Jannie van Wyk who generously lent us his beautiful Cessna 210.

Heartfelt thanks too to Martin Meyer of Navigators, for taking me on roads in the Cederberg that I couldn't imagine conquering in my little car and for the delicious campsite meals! To Gerrit and Chantal Karsten of Cederberg Oasis for the warm bed, food and stories. And to Quinton and Nicole Martins for becoming such good friends and for helping me to find the elusive Cedar tree.

Thanks must also be given to Struik for the opportunity – especially to Dominique le Roux and Samantha Menezes-Fick for the freedom and trust. To Martin Jones at Hirt & Carter for making everything so easy. To Agfa for generous contribution to film, Greg Stopforth for loaning me his darkroom and for patient help with Lith printing, and to my parents, Chrissie and Peter Cowling, for caring and for always checking that I wasn't lost. To Karena du Plessis for having faith in me to share this project with her – it has been an honour and a pleasure.

To Jock Kannemeyer, for carrying my tripod without complaint, for generously sharing some of the adventure and making it more fun, for being my own private helicopter pilot and for lifting me into the sky.

Vanessa Cowling

Map Key
Small Town
Large Village
Village
Place of interest / Farm
Nature Reserve / Park
MOUNTAIN RANGE
Water Body
ATLANTIC OCEAN
Bitterfontein
Nuwerus
BOKKEVELD
Sout
Klein -Doring
Brandkop
Hantam
Nieuwoudtville
R 27
Grootdrif
R 27
Koekenaap
Lutzville
Vanrhynsdorp
Vredendal
R 27
Klawer
Doringbaai
Trawal
Pakhuis Pass
Pakhuis
Lambert's Bay
Graafwater
Clanwilliam
Clanwilliam Dam
Leipoldtville
CEDERBERG
Wupperthal
Sandberg
Elands Bay
Nieuwoudt Pass
R 27
Olifants River
Doring
Dwarsrivier
Citrusdal
Piekenierskloof Pass
Dwarskersbos
Aurora
PIKETBERG
St Helena Bay
Stompneus Bay
St Helena Bay
Laaiplek
Paternoster
Port Owen
Velddrif
Cape Columbine
Geodverwacht
Piketberg
Vredenburg
Wittewater
Berg River
R44
Porterville
R79
Langebaanweg
Saldanha
Koringberg
Groot Winterhoek Wilderness Area
West Coast Fossil Park
Hopefield
Saldanha Bay
Donkergat
Langebaan
Postberg Nature Reserve
Langebaan Lagoon
Moorreesburg
Kraalbaai
Geelbek Environmental Education Centre
Churchhaven
Geelbek
R45
N 7
West Coast National Park
R27
KASTEELBERG
Riebeek-Wes
Riebeek-Kasteel
Yzerfontein
Darling
Hermon
Dassen Island
Oudepost Farm
Malmesbury
Ganzekraal
Mamre
Atlantis
Melkbosstrand
N 1

Contents

The West Coast 8
from the Cederberg to the sea

Fields of green and gold 12
Riebeek Valley, Yzerfontein, Darling

Sand, sea and sky 52
Langebaan, West Coast National Park, Churchhaven, Saldanha, Paternoster, Velddrif

Harvest fields 100
Goedverwacht, Wittewater, Aurora, Piketberg, Hopefield, Porterville

Mountain majesty 148
Citrusdal, The Cederberg, Langkloof, Eselbank, Wupperthal, Clanwilliam, Elands Bay, Lambert's Bay

Glossary 200

West Coast Annual Events 202

Index 204

The West Coast

from the Cederberg to the sea

Introduction

There's plenty of time to think on the way up the West Coast when you're stuck behind an enormous truck with the slogan *Moving Grain is our Game* emblazoned across its rear end. But then, there's plenty of time to think on the West Coast generally. It's that kind of place. There's all the space you might need with huge expanses of sky, stunning sunsets and plenty of room to breathe. Perfect!

And – depending on your mood and inclination – you can access the West Coast via two very different routes that I've attempted to capture in this book. If it's the sand, sea and wheeling seabirds you're after, then you can take the coast road – the R27 – which affords you a very particular sense of the area as you head up past Yzerfontein, the West Coast National Park and on to towns such as Langebaan and Velddrif. Be sure to roll down your car window when you get near the wide windswept beaches. The smell of the ocean is intoxicating. But, if it's soft rolling hills and vistas of sheep, vineyards and windmills your heart craves, then take the N7 inland and you'll drive through quaint country towns with their own unique charms.

One day, somewhere in between Lambert's Bay, Graafwater and Piketberg, I waved at three other bakkies as they whizzed by in the other direction. After about an hour and a half of solitary driving I began to worry. Was I on the right road? Where were all the other people? And then I reminded myself that this was the West Coast and absolutely as it should be – no crowds, no great rush and plenty to look at. So, I stopped panicking and settled down to try to find a house that was made by earlier farmers out of old whale bones that had washed up on the shore. I couldn't find the house, but it didn't really seem to matter. The sun was out, the flowers on the side of the road were a brilliant orange and the open road lay before me.

The West Coast also seems to be a good place to find yourself or rediscover what's really important to you. There's a pared-down sparseness to the landscape, which demands a degree of barefaced honesty that you can ignore in other areas that might be more overtly beautiful, or more full of distraction. It's these qualities that draw people up the coast – and exactly what has kept families farming there for countless generations.

But for all its apparent barrenness, the West Coast is an area unbelievably rich in history and natural resources. The rock art in the Cederberg, the fossils at the West Coast Fossil Park, the harvest from the sea, and the amazing flowers that make over the landscape each spring are just the beginnings of what you'll find up here if you take the trouble to look.

And then, of course, there are the people. Living in a city it's easy to forget your shared humanity in the daily grind. You fight for parking, jostle in supermarket queues and sit for hours in traffic that might take you to a job you don't love. Up the West Coast it's different. Once you're out of Cape Town's ever-spreading sprawl and have Table Mountain firmly behind you, things begin to change. For starters everybody on the West Coast seems to have a *bynaam* or nickname, usually infused with humour. I met a Bokkompie – son of a *bokkoms* baron near Velddrif, a Boontjies – a guy who grew an excellent crop of Sandveld beans each year and Duimpie – a fisherman who had lost his thumb out at sea.

Once I shot past a farm that had dams bristling with *waterblommetjies* – exactly what I needed for this book. So I pulled in and with all the bravado of a woman on a mission asked the farmer if he would be prepared to sell me some *waterblommetjies* for the book I was working on.

'Sure,' Chris van Niekerk replied with an enormous smile, 'but if you want them today, then you'll have to go in and get them and, I can assure you, the water is *baie koud*. But, why don't you come back and we'll have picked some for you and my mom can make you a *waterblommetjie-bredie*. She uses all the old West Coast recipes.'

In the city you don't generally go back for things. And you rarely drive nearly two hours to try again. You would normally just move on to another shop, another service provider and get what you wanted immediately without any fuss. The *waterblommetjies* proved to be a good learning curve. I went back for them and Isobel van Niekerk made an outstanding *bredie* and I spent the better part of the day with a woman who knows and loves the *veld* with a quiet passion that is hard to ignore. I kept wondering why they would invite a total stranger back into their home and go to so much trouble for a person they didn't know. But then I remembered that this was a West Coast trait.

Throughout the area I have been fed and given copious cups of tea while people took out their old photos, showed me around their homes and farms and shared their family treasures, secrets and recipes. It will be impossible ever to think of this area as barren or empty again.

But for all the kindness and generosity I encountered, it would be naïve to imagine that the West Coast is devoid of troubles. Unemployment, poverty and alcohol abuse are enormous problems up the coast. They're not isolated to these areas, but at times communities seemed quite ravaged. Perhaps it's the raw sun, wind and rain that made them appear that much more vulnerable. There was also a huge disparity between the old folks and the younger generation. The elderly people were amazing – hard working, God-fearing and independent. But there were so many households headed up by women in their 60s and 70s who were tasked with raising a squad of grandchildren. Many of their own children had died – of HIV/AIDS-related illnesses or violence – while others had just fallen through the cracks and were drinking themselves to death. One old man was slaving away while his son lay in a wreck of a car in the yard smoking an enormous joint. Why didn't his children help him in his manual labour seemed an obvious question. His reply, 'One is off his head, the other is sick all the time.'

Of course there are West Coast regrets. There wasn't enough time to watch the seasons change in the wheat fields and watch them turn from green to gold and then to a singed grey at the end of summer. There wasn't enough time to go Cape Gannet counting in the Velddrif area with the avid birdwatchers up there, or to collect kelp to make kelp pickle at Paternoster. There wasn't nearly enough time to cure olives picked in the Riebeek Valley or to follow every mountain track in the Cederberg or to go surfing at Elands Bay. Certainly – and most disappointingly of all – there was not enough time for all the stories and characters.

For one particular week I moved up to the West Coast and settled in at the historic farm of Kersefontein near Hopefield where the wildly entertaining Julian Melck lives and farms. I also took along two frisky horses, figuring it would be impossible to be away so long and leave them stuck in town. The horses had a blast on the farm – cows, sheep, pigs, springbok and ostriches for city horses are always a novelty – but I soon ran out of food. One rainy day on my way to a farmer's co-op in Vredenburg I passed an old *boer* sitting in his *bakkie*. On the back were bales of lucerne – just what I was looking for. I stopped and asked him if he would sell me some bales. He agreed and said I should come back to his farm with the blue roof later that afternoon on my way back from whatever adventure I was going to have. I did but the old man wasn't there and I found his son working out back. Not only was the farmer selling me extremely hard-to-come-by feed, but he was charging me exactly what he had paid for it. Clearly madness in the eyes of his son.

As I was leaving I passed the farmer on the road and he invited me to stop and turn around – he had also put out some mealies for my horses. He also said that he wanted to write a book and was keen to tell me his stories. One of my greatest regrets is that I never did manage to find the time to go back and meet up again with Meneer Laubscher. His stories were probably exactly what I was looking for, rich with West Coast humour and wisdom. Hopefully one day I will be back. Only, second time round it will be with more patience and less haste.

The musician Zirk Bergh wrote about the West Coast: *'Ons het baie perlemoen, Lekker dik galjoen, Rooi gekookte krewe, Dis die lekker lewe, Hier op die Weskus.'*

That pretty much says it all.

Previous spread *The West Coast is a tapestry of colours and textures made up of mussel shells on the beach, mountains, ploughed fields and a splash of yellow canola.*

Fields of green and gold

Riebeek Valley, Yzerfontein, Darling

The Swartland has wonderfully fertile soil that, year after year, produces bountiful crops of grain, grapes and olives. This area also gave rise to some of the country's history makers. Jan Christiaan Smuts and Daniël François Malan were both born and raised in the Riebeek Valley and, whether or not you agree with their politics, they helped shape the development of South Africa. Today, the country villages are being discovered by city folk keen to escape the rat race.

Riebeek Valley and surrounds

The two little Riebeek villages – Riebeek-Kasteel and Riebeek-Wes – are less than an hour's drive from Cape Town along the N7 and then the R46. The view over the Riebeek Valley always comes as something of a surprise. On the unremarkable climb up the back of the Kasteelberg, the imposing mountain that looms over the dorpies below, during the winter months you glide through shimmering green wheat fields. On a stormy day you might catch a glimpse of a classic picture that speaks of life in the country, and rural bliss: a windmill, a simple reservoir, blackening rain clouds and white, white sheep standing in a field of emerald.

You'll pass historic old farms such as Modderfontein, Doornkloof and Meerhof right at the top. The road bends, you're through the road cutting and – wow! There it is. The view ... a sweep of vineyards, olive groves, a church spire and the blue Klein Drakenstein mountains to the north-east. Behind these, standing tall and proud, is yet another row of majestic and formidable rock forms. This is the Swartland, or Black Land.

There's some debate how the region got its name. It could have been after the indigenous *renosterbos*, which turns black during the winter rains. Another possibility is that when the first explorers reached what is now Malmesbury, they dug into the fertile land around the mineral spring and found rich, black soil. Both are evocative explanations for a beautiful part of the West Coast.

The two towns nestled in the valley are Riebeek-Kasteel and Riebeek-Wes. Riebeek-Kasteel is named after the mountain – the Kasteelberg or Castle Mountain – that stands sentinel over the towns. The naming of the mountain can be traced back to the 1660s when Pieter Cruythoff and his men made one of the first European expeditions to the area. They were tasked with trading with the Khoi and reclaiming stolen livestock. The men set up camp on the lower slopes of the mountain and Pieter Meerhof, second-in-command and designated journal writer of the expedition, climbed the mountain and named it Riebeek's Kasteel after the first commander of the Cape, Jan van Riebeeck.

The towns are five kilometres apart. The two communities each wanted their own churches, which is why two separate towns developed around them. Today the valley is peaceful, although it wasn't always so. In the early days of the Colony, there was deep-seated and violent enmity between the European settlers and the indigenous tribes who had been living in the area for many centuries before the burghers arrived. In 1700 Governor van der Stel failed to keep his word to the head of the Cochoqua tribe, Mgonnemoa, with unhappy consequences. The Governor had promised the tribal leader that the valley would be reserved for the exclusive use of the Cochoquas and Koekeman-Sonquas, but in that year Van der Stel granted permission to a few free burghers to farm in the area, pushing the boundary between the settlers and indigenous people further north.

Previous spread *The 'Cape Breadbasket': extensive fields of grain are typical of the areas around Malmesbury, Porterville, Moorreesburg and the aptly-named Koringberg.*

This spread *The picturesque Riebeek Valley is home to a growing number of city folk.*

an influx of artists,

wanting a differe

writers and people
way of life

Skirmishes followed as the Dutch East India Company became more determined to claim the fertile valley for their own use as a grazing post for the flocks that supported the growing settlement at the Cape, and the tribes retaliated to the betrayal by stealing the burghers' cattle and sheep. 'Zonquasdrift' is a reminder of one of the clashes between the two groups and marks the place where the Sonquas were forced back over the Berg River. Revenge – further stock theft and the burning of Allesverloren farm in 1704 – followed.

But trouble didn't just come in the form of angry indigenous people. During the early 1700s, the Riebeek Valley attracted a motley crew of runaway slaves, deserting soldiers, criminals and rebels. Much like the *drosters* who disappeared into the caves near Cape Hangklip in the Overberg, so too these outcasts found refuge in the wilderness of the valley.

However, according to Willem Smuts, a retired *gemengde boer* from the district and a relative of the famous Boer general and statesman Jan Christiaan Smuts, 'When the British arrived in 1795 and the Cape Colony fell under their control, a new and modern era dawned. The British administration was enlightened and new trade opportunities opened up. Property rights were enshrined and wine farms in the area prospered.

'To illustrate just how good things were for the valley's farmers, it's worth remembering one of my forefathers, Michiel Nicolaas Smuts,' Willem explains over a cup of tea on a late autumn afternoon. 'In October 1813 he paid 533 rix-dollars for the farm Ongegund, which was later known as Boplaas. In five years, he had planted 50 000 vines, had made 20 leagues (or 'leaguer', which is approximately 577 litres, or 127 gallons) of wine, had a harvest of oats and barley and had produced 200 sacks of wheat. Just eight years later, Michiel was even wealthier. By then his vineyards expanded to 70 000 vines and produced 70 leagues of wine and he harvested 400 sacks of wheat. In 1834, after the abolition of slavery, things were tougher because farmers didn't have free or cheap labour.'

Twenty years ago life in these two sleepy hamlets was quite different from what it is today. It was largely Afrikaans and almost exclusively agricultural. But then, when jaded city dwellers discovered just how easy it was to commute from the hurly-burly of skyscrapers and traffic jams, they began buying up old houses and the village culture started to change. More people now speak English than ever before, little bistros and restaurants have opened up and shopping has become more than a trip to the farmers' co-op.

One long-time resident of the valley recalls some of the changes she has seen over the last two decades. 'The two towns were quite competitive,' she says with a laugh. 'The only time we used to get together was for the annual agricultural show, which was held at the show grounds in Riebeek-Wes. The competition was really fierce and the two villages would be pitted against each other. Back then there were only two English families in the valley. That's changed as more *Engels* have moved in.

Now there's an influx of artists, writers and people wanting a different way of life. It's good. Lots of B&Bs have opened up and people come out for the weekends to enjoy what we often take for granted. The two agricultural societies have combined and that says a lot in small towns like these! The suspicion between English and Afrikaans residents has also disappeared. There's a quiz evening once a month at L'Attitude restaurant and everyone goes. It sounds funny, but a decade ago that wouldn't have happened!'

This spread *Each year the Olive Festival in Riebeek-Kasteel and Riebeek-Wes attracts thousands of visitors keen to taste the region's delicious olive products and enjoy a slice of country life. Junior drum majorettes from the small mission station of Goedverwacht march through town and entertain the crowds with their deft moves and well-rehearsed steps.*

Jan Smuts – son of the Riebeek Valley

Jan Christiaan Smuts was born in 1870 on the farm Ongegund near Riebeek-Wes. He was a man of prodigious intellect, inquiring mind and far-reaching thinking. This led him to question the Afrikaners' future in a changing South Africa – a debate that won him both friends and plenty of enemies. He's been described as a statesman, a soldier, a naturalist and a philosopher.

Jan Smuts studied law at Stellenbosch and Cambridge Universities and returned to South Africa in the 1890s where he became the state attorney of Johannesburg and a member of Paul Kruger's government.

As a young man, it's believed he contributed to the book *Een Eeu van Onrecht* (*A Century of Wrong*), outlining how the Boers suffered at the hands of the British. During the Second Boer War (1899–1902) he was a commandant in the Boer Army, engaging in guerrilla attacks against the British.

This spread *Johan Vlok from the farm Môrester has been farming in the Riebeek Valley for generations and produces everything from vegetables, to grapes and olives.*

But, contradictorily, he also believed that South Africa's future lay with co-operation with the outside world and Britain in particular, and it was this reconciliatory attitude that influenced subsequent decisions, infuriating many Afrikaners. By 1908, it was believed that Smuts had rejected some of the fundamentalism that went with his nationality and turned his back on his Boer roots.

Smuts' decision not to reprieve Jopie Fourie (the only rebel executed after the failed Boer rebellion of 1914–1915), his close friendship with Winston Churchill and his appointment as honorary Field Marshal in the British Army in September 1941 enraged his detractors.

Smuts eventually alienated popular vote to such a degree that he lost in the critical 1948 elections, which brought the National Party under the leadership of Daniël François Malan (who grew up on Allesverloren farm just down the road from Ongegund) to power. It's hard to imagine what South Africa's path would have been if Jan Smuts and the United Party had won the vote, rather than the architects of apartheid.

The Smuts legacy lives on

Growing up a Smuts wasn't easy in an Afrikaans *dorpie* over six decades ago, when most of the residents believed that Jan Christiaan had sold out to the British.

'*Ek moes altyd pad gee vir die ander kinders. Maar ek het geleer om vol te hou*,' remembers Willem, who lives just a short distance from the farm *Ongegund* where Jan Smuts was born.

Until not so long ago he was a farmer in the district, but now his son works the farm and he lives in town with his wife. There is a telescope mounted in the kitchen looking onto the adjacent hectares, which Willem bought and stocked with springbok. The large piece of land in the middle of town is an anomaly, but then much of small town practice defies city logic. The *veld* teems with birds and small mammals and while it's not exactly the same as living on an enormous farm with far-off horizons, it has certainly helped make the transition into town that much easier.

Willem is a collector of memories and old photos. He has a black and white photograph of a span of mules working in the wheat fields. Because of the crude machinery, it looks like a picture from the turn of the previous century but Willem points out that people in the district farmed with teams of animals until the 1950s.

'So much has happened in the last hundred years,' says the old man sagely. 'Today with all our technology we think we are so clever. I keep this photograph as a reminder of where we came from. You need to look back to get your bearings. That way, you can go forward with integrity.'

Integrity or *eerbaarheid* features strongly in any Smuts household. After all, Jan Christiaan risked enormous censure for flying in the face of popular Afrikaner opinion at the time, and this characteristic seems to run through the family's veins.

'My older sister married Jannie Stals, one of the first cabinet ministers in D.F. Malan's government, and I used to hear of some of the things that went on in parliament. On the strength of that I decided I would never get involved in politics. When I was growing up I decided that I would always strive to be independent and *selfstandig*. I never want to be on anybody's payroll.'

Willem has a curious piece of paper with the following information about Smuts jotted on it. He cannot remember where he got it, but one can only imagine that these are the cryptic notes of an anxious hostess jotting hurried pointers about the famous man in order to make sure that his stay was as pleasant as possible:

J.C. Smuts
'no mixed grill'
no smoker
very simple taste – home cooked meals
fond of children (after dinner mints)
no alcohol – preferred beer

And then there's a series of strange words and their explanations, which are even harder to fathom:

Boeregeregte
Kaboemmielies – stampmielies
Spioenpap – beskuit
Doopgooiers – hardboiled eggs
Hertzoggies – appelkoos konfytkoekies
Uitlander reën – rice
Koringkoffie – swart koffie sonder suiker
Maagbomme – sousboontjies

This spread *It's a dog's life! Abel Daniels is busy clearing old vines from Môrester fields while his faithful hound settles down in the dirt to wait for his master. The Riebeek Valley is wonderfully fertile and supports a wide variety of crops. Some of the red wine vines in the valley are infected with* rolblaar, *a common virus that turns the leaves a vivid red in autumn.*

I am struggling to capture the light of the olive. It is silver – sometimes more blue, sometimes greenish, bronze, off white, on a ground of yellow, pink, violet or orange to red ochre. But it is very difficult. Very difficult.

– Vincent van Gogh

Malmesbury *bry*

Almost everybody in South Africa knows about the Malmesbury *bry* (pronounced 'bray') or burr. It's unmistakable when you hear it, but difficult to mimic if you didn't grow up in the area.

Professor Frank Hendricks from the University of the Western Cape's Afrikaans department explains: '*Bry* occurs when the pronunciation of the r-sound is characterised by the vibration of the uvula. For example, when a sentence such as *Môre, Meneer, ek kom van Moorreesburg af* is uttered, all the r-sounds come from the back of the throat.'

He goes on to say; 'Many people associate the *bry* with towns in the Swartland district such as Malmesbury, Moorreesburg and Hopefield, but linguistic/dialectic research shows that there are other areas as well where *bry* is an everyday phenomenon. These include the Overberg (Caledon and Bredasdorp), the Sandveld, and the southern Free State (Ficksburg and Winburg).'

But it seems a *bry* is not just a *bry*. According to Prof. Hendricks, each area produces its own distinctive *bry*-variant, so much so that one is permitted to speak of the Sandveld, Swartland, Overberg or Southern Free State *bry*.

While each *bry*-variant might be pretty distinctive, how they developed is nowhere near as clear. But it doesn't really matter. The *bry* gives a warm lilt to country speech and illustrates just how rich and textured the Afrikaans language is.

Extra virgin olive oil – The most sought-after and flavoursome form, this comes from the first pressing of the olives, when the oil is extracted without the use of heat or chemicals.

This spread *Olives thrive in the Riebeek Valley and ripen in the summer heat.*

Kloovenburg

Kloovenburg, at the entrance to Riebeek-Kasteel, was one of the Cape's first farms, established over 300 years ago. In the Du Toit family for the past 50 years, it produces outstanding wines and top quality olive oil.

Annalene du Toit is responsible for the olive groves, some of the first in the region. Married to Pieter du Toit, the farm's heir and winemaker, she downplays her achievements, but her products are sought after in delis around the country.

Kloovenburg's olive oil and products are much more than a small home industry. In 2005, after only four years in production, the Kloovenburg Estate 2004 Extra Virgin Olive Oil was voted as the world's best certified extra virgin olive oil, while the estate was recognised as one of the top 15 extra virgin olive oil producers in the world.

'This award is very special to us,' says Annalene. 'We believe it will not only assist in promoting Kloovenburg, but will also aid the establishment of South Africa's reputation as a producer of top quality extra virgin olive oil both nationally and internationally.'

According to Annalene, for excellent extra virgin olive oil, the oil needs to be pressed within 24 hours of harvesting. Centrifugal force in the olive press immediately separates the oil from bulk product, thereby minimising further deterioration.

But Kloovenburg doesn't just produce excellent olive oil. There are tapenades, olive jams, dipping oils and now even olive oil-based body products to choose from. Annalene and her youngest son, Daniel, are the products developers. 'A lot of experimenting is done for each product,' she laughs. 'Starting in my kitchen, Daniel, who is six, is my chief taster.

'If he doesn't like it, I stop right there. If he likes it I continue experimenting and everybody helps to taste, from friends and family to the farm secretaries. I love experimenting with all kinds of food anyway so it's not a chore but rather something I enjoy.'

Olive Boutique's Cure

Michael and Juliana Meredith from the Olive Boutique encourage people to cure their own olives. It's easy to do and fun. You can buy the olives from them (and other farms) in season and get creative with what you add to the final mix – a touch of lemon, garlic and herbs. 'It's simple,' reassures Michael. 'You just have to follow the steps.'

This spread *Curing your own olives is easy and a fun way to bring a little country life into your kitchen*

A 5l clean plastic bucket with a tight fitting lid
3kg black olives, either Mission or Kalamata
Fresh clean water
Salt (buy salt that does not have any additives like corn starch; we use coarse sea salt)

Wash the olives and put them into the bucket – don't be tempted to put more than 3kg in a bucket, as it is important that there is enough space left for lots of liquid. Prepare at least 3l of a 10 percent salt solution (1kg salt to 10l of water). Make sure all the salt is dissolved.

Put the bucket in a place where it won't matter if spillage occurs; the kitchen sink works fine. Fill the bucket to the brim with the salt solution and let it overflow. Fasten the lid, making sure that there is no air left in the bucket as an air pocket will encourage the growth of mould.

Put the bucket (it may leak so be careful where you put it) in a cool place. After two weeks empty the olives into your kitchen sink and rinse them. Don't be concerned if there is white scum. For the technically minded, this is lactic acid, a by-product of the fermentation.

Using a sharp blade cut a slit in each olive and put them back into the cleaned bucket. Make up a fresh salt solution, fill the bucket, then seal. Put it back into the cool place for four more weeks. Open the bucket carefully and taste an olive. If it is still bitter they are not ready. Replace the lid and check again in another week.

Once the olives are ready – their taste is to your liking – take them out of the salt water and bottle them in your favourite dressing. We bottle some in salt water, some in flavoured vinegar, and some in a mixture of brine and vinegar. The bottles must be clean, sterile and airtight. Preserved correctly these olives will last for years, although if you have followed the instructions they will be so nice that your family and friends won't let you keep them that long.

For the Lord your God is bringing you into a good land, a land of brooks of water, of fountains and springs, flowing out in the valleys and hills, a land of wheat and barley, of vines and fig trees and pomegranates, a land of olive trees and honey ...

Deuteronomy 8: 7-8

Allesverloren

It's autumn and the vineyards of Allesverloren have turned their signature ruby red. The panoramic view over the burnished vines is a painter's dream. As you squeeze a generous glob of your Winsor & Newton oils onto your palette, you'll be hard pressed to decide where to stop: Scarlet Lake, Cadmium Red, Vermilion Hue, Raw Sienna, Carmine or Rose Madder Genuine? And, if there's snow on the distant peaks, it's picture postcard perfect.

Two minutes from Riebeek-Kasteel, the farm dates back to 1704 and – like most things in the Swartland – has a story attached to it. In 1696, the Governor of the Cape, Willem Adriaan van der Stel, gave the farm to widow Cloete – a courageous woman and one of the first people to settle in what then would have been the inhospitable Swartland. The unofficial or *skinder* story is that Van der Stel was keen to give farms to widows throughout the colony for a number of reasons. Not only did many of them prove to be resourceful farmers, but he was also ensured of good company and a convivial bed when he set out on his travels.

Widow Cloete didn't have an easy time of it, however, and after one trip to the *nagmaal* in Stellenbosch, which took her the best part of two weeks, she returned to find that the local tribe, the Koekeman-Sonquas, had burned down her farm and stolen all her cattle. You only have to imagine her feelings of despair and hopelessness when she arrived to see her farmhouse in ruins and everything pillaged. She's reputed to have called out, '*allesverloren*' or 'all is lost'.

The name stuck and it was registered at the beginning of the 1700s. However, today the farm's prospects are far from gloomy. Bought by the Malan family in 1872, it has been passed down the years to the sons. The family names of Daniël François and Stephanus François have also been passed down the generations and consequently all the men in the family are known – a little irreverently – as either Danie or Fanie.

But it's not always been the eldest son who has inherited the valuable property. Daniël François, second generation Malan on Allesverloren, was far more interested in the church and politics and his father, annoyed by his heir's apparent lack of interest in farming, bypassed him, giving the farm instead to his younger brother, Stephanus François, who developed the estate into a Port-producing farm. And what of Daniël François? More commonly known as D.F., he went on to become the leader of the National Party and served as prime minister of South Africa from 1948 to 1954.

Allesverloren is probably best known for its delicious Port, which is a nutty, raisiny blend of a number of Portuguese varietals – Tinta Barocca, Souzão, Pontac, Malvasia Rey, Tinta Röritz, Tinta Francisca and Touriga Naçional. The Port vines are over 40 years old and each vineyard block is planted with a mix of vines so that the grapes are already blended when they're harvested. There are individual blocks of grapes as well, and in the last few years Danie has produced some great single varietal wines. His Shiraz is a winner, as is the Tinta Barocca.

This spread *During autumn a corner of the Riebeek Valley looks like a patchwork quilt of complementary reds and greens. Each season gives rise to a different rhythm and the landscape changes depending on what's happening on the farms. Many of the estates have been in the same families for generations and were some of the first established in the Cape Colony.*

Ansie Vlok's quince jelly

Ansie Vlok has been living in the Riebeek Valley for more years than she cares to remember but the farm has been in her husband's family for generations. She loves their farm Môrester, which looks out onto the mountains and has a sense of unlimited space and sky. Ansie's best time of the day is the late afternoon or early evening when she takes some time to relax and walk around the farm. She has a favourite route that makes a big loop through the farm and the two little villages.

Ansie's quince jelly is sought after. It's brilliant amber, clear and shimmering much like a jewel, and is delicious scooped onto bread, toast, or scones, or as an accompaniment to pork dishes. You might also be tempted to eat it straight out of the jar!

'You must only use fruit that is just ripe,' advises Ansie. 'If you use very ripe fruit, you can make a plan but the jelly won't be as nice. If you've got your own quince tree, the fruit is ready to pick when the first quince falls to the ground. Then you need to get busy.'

This spread *Ansie Vlok has been making her famous quince jelly for years. It's a slow process, but well worth every glistening mouthful. The jelly is delicious with meat and cheese.*

Peel and cut 2kg quinces into pieces and put them in a stainless steel pot with 2,5l water. Simmer for about 1 hour. Secure a piece of cheesecloth or something similar over a bucket or big pot and tip the cooked quince into the cloth so that the juice can drip through. It's very important that you don't stir the quince mixture, or try to squeeze the juice through the cloth. It must drip through by itself, otherwise your jelly won't be so clear.

For every 500ml quince juice, add 400g sugar. Heat through until it's boiling rapidly and cook the jelly for about 1½ to 2 hours. To test if it's ready, put a little on a saucer and put this in the fridge to see if a gel forms.

If you've got a jam thermometer the jelly will be ready when it reaches 105°C, and should be a deep red wine colour. Skim off any foam or impurities and bottle while it's still warm. Put the lids on and turn the bottles upside down so that they seal properly.

Enjoy!

the oily, com
of lanolin h

Bartholomeus Klip Farmhouse

The smell from the sheep-shearing shed is pungent and earthy. It hits you as you round the corner. There is an evocative tang that reminds you of dusty gravel roads, red-roofed farmhouses and *klomps* of blue-gum trees. First off, it's the smell of wet woollen jerseys on a damp winter's day. Next is the oily, comforting smell of lanolin hand-cream, and then the muttony smell of live, thrashing animals crowded into a packed shed. It's spring and sheep-shearing season at Bartholomeus Klip, a working wheat and sheep farm in the Riebeek Valley, just over an hour from Cape Town, and a ten-minute drive from the sleepy hamlet of Hermon.

The shearers work at lightning speed. A wooden gate is swung open, the animals clatter onto the raised platform and before you can say, 'mint sauce', they're on their backs or sides having their fleecy jackets removed. The fleece is tossed down onto long tables where it's graded and cleaned of all the really dirty, grungy bits and then packed into bales. There are a few nicks along the way, the bright red standing out against the creamy wool, but the aim is to work fast without injuring the animals and these are shearers who pride themselves on being able to shear 25 to 30 sheep in an hour. It's backbreaking work and the wiry shearers are sweating.

Outside in the weak spring sunshine, a group of sheepdogs lies in wait for action; there is no dozing off for these working dogs. They snap at the flies buzzing around. One dog has mismatched eyes and an engaging expression. Imagining these dogs in a suburban garden is absurd. They're made to move and do – purpose-driven dogs all the way.

Bartholomeus Klip isn't all sheep and wheat, however. It's also a fabulous getaway, as the old farmhouse has been converted into luxurious accommodation and is in the middle of 4 000ha of rare renosterveld (*see* information *opposite* about the Elandsberg Nature Reserve). Converting the farmhouse into a luxury retreat was the brainchild of the late Dale Parker. He was, according to family lore, a man with enormous vision and a willingness to take risks when others would quietly retreat and whom his wife, Elizabeth, describes as 'nothing short of a hero'. He lies buried on the farm and from his simple grave there is a great view that on a clear day stretches all the way to Table Mountain. Unlike many other wealthy men, *Meneer* Parker is not buried in his Sunday best – he's in his work clothes, with his old boots on and the bits and bobs that were found in his pocket on the day he died in 2001. In short, he was a man of the people and the soil.

Life at Bartholomeus Klip wasn't always so genteel, however. In the early 1700s, when farmers were only beginning to move to these outlying areas of the Cape Colony, the elderly immigrant Frantz Joosten van der Lubstadt settled on the farm with his vivacious young wife, Maria Mouton. According to old court records, it was an unhappy marriage, with an even unhappier outcome. He was much older than she, reputedly stingy and regularly abusive. In January 1714, things came to a head when two farm workers, Titus Bengale and Fortuijn of Angola, came to Maria's rescue during a domestic dispute.

They beat the old man to death with a plough scraper and crammed his body in a porcupine hole. It's not clear whether Titus of Bengal, as he was also known, was Maria's lover at the time of the murder or became

forting smell and-cream

her paramour soon after the murder, but they had a relationship for three years. Frantz's death went unnoticed until a visitor to the farm noted Frantz's absence and discovered what had happened. Reports differ in the details but all three were tried, given the death penalty and died agonising deaths after being tortured. The heads of the two men were then cut off and mounted on stakes. This served two purposes. It acted as a cautionary warning to other slaves who were railing against their owners, and sent out a clear message to settlers' wives who found their husbands less than attractive.

Elandsberg Nature Reserve

Elizabeth Parker is passionate about conservation and continues working to ensure that this valuable piece of Western Cape heritage isn't lost to the plough. This nature reserve, situated at the farm, has been the subject of numerous studies – and even a lawsuit!

She explains more about the vision she and her husband, Dale, shared: 'The Elandsberg Nature Reserve (Bartholomeus Klip is on land owned by Elandsberg Farms) is a highly sensitive and ecologically important stretch of land, the botanical value of which is incalculable.'

What makes it so special? Well, it's the largest conserved portion of West Coast *renosterveld* left in the Cape Lowlands. This highly threatened vegetation type has been almost entirely ploughed up for wheat farming, and less than 3% now exists in its natural state. It is rich in plant species, among them many beautiful bulbs. The checklist of plant species recorded on the farm now numbers around 800.

'Dozens of rare and endangered plant species are found at Elandsberg, including two that occur only on the farm itself,' continues Elizabeth.

'These are the Elandsberg candelabra lily (*Brunsivia elandsmontana*) which was named only in 2000 and produces, in autumn, a dainty head of small, lily-like flowers the colour of crushed strawberries. The diminutive Elandsberg pea (*Lotononis prostrata*) was first described in 1990 and bears sweetpea-like flowers of a beautiful, wisteria blue.

Ranked in terms of biodiversity criteria, Elandsberg (together with the adjoining Voëlvlei area) has been identified as the highest priority area within the entire Swartland/Boland *renosterveld* area. It was named as the most important conservation area of West Coast *renosterveld* in 1996. The land in question is well known as the last remaining viable habitat of the geometric tortoise, the world's second most endangered land tortoise.'

Luckily for us – and future generations – the farm has a history of dedicated commitment to conservation by its owners. As far back as 1971 the then owner, the late Dale Parker, initiated the declaration of the *fynbos* area as a private nature reserve, and began the reintroduction of game such as eland, springbok, bontebok and black wildebeest. In 1989 it became a Natural Heritage Site under the South African Natural Heritage Programme and this means it is protected from development.

Following spread *On a stormy winter's day when the rain has been lashing the Cape, Grotto Bay is a moody painting in blue, grey and silver. Pull on your raincoat and go for a walk along the pebbly coast. Your cheeks will turn red in the wind, and you'll come back invigorated.*

Yzerfontein and surrounds

On a late Saturday morning, the informal fish market just outside the small holiday village of Yzerfontein is doing a roaring trade in fresh snoek. The boats pull in, the fish auctioneers start calling their prices and before you know it, you have a fish in the back of your car for tonight's braai.

Just under 100km from Cape Town, Yzerfontein is a popular weekend getaway for Capetonians, but in the winter months the holiday mansions are deserted and the gulls hold sway. This is the time to explore the backroads of the area.

Ganzekraal

The handsome homestead of Ganzekraal is no longer standing, but about 50km outside Cape Town on the R27 you'll see a signpost pointing to Ganzekraal. The highway slices through what used to be an enormous farm with the house built up on the right and a beach cottage, Seaspray, near the water. If you take the turn-off pointing toward the sea, what you'll find today is a pretty cove with a group of cottages run by the West Coast municipality. It's a good place to holiday but there's nothing to remind us of the old farm that encompassed this area, or the family that loved it so dearly.

After Mary Melck Kuttel died in 1977, her daughter, Frances Keegan, found a manuscript her mother had written about growing up on Ganzekraal and she edited, illustrated and published *Ganzekraal – A West Coast Year*, a record of a very different West Coast life. Ganzekraal was much like the other historic homesteads in the area, Groote Post, Geelbek, Oesterwal, Buck Bay: big, generous whitewashed homes that housed expanding families entrepreneurial enough to risk their fortunes up the West Coast.

Here, children's days were spent exploring the dunes, helping on the farm or disappearing until sunset investigating isolated coves. It's a childhood that unfortunately seems lost to most of us today.

Mary remembers her mother's formidable energy and the care that went to ensuring the family and staff were well fed throughout the year. She writes, 'She had a busy day supervising the storing of a boatload of snoek which had been brought up from Jacob's Bay the day before. The fish had already been rough-salted; a hundred had been cleaned, headed and split open with a stick inserted across the top to keep the fish flat. These were then hung in the sun to dry. Towards evening they were brought into the storeroom and they would be hung out every fine day and brought in at night until thoroughly cured. The rest of the fish was cut up into *mootjies* (fillets), salted and laid in shallow vats.

'Mother regarded the state of the *pakhuis* with satisfaction when the last *mootjie* was put in the barrel. The flitches of bacon hanging from the rafters and strings of dried harders at the end of the snoek racks had been much amplified by this good haul of snoek, which had been caught off Dassen Island. She was sorry that it was no longer possible to get a box of penguin eggs from the island, although we children would only eat the yolk – the pale sea-green jelly which took the place of the white egg (egg white) seemed to us too fishy in flavour.

'Sometimes we would run over to Jacob's Bay and beg a couple of crayfish tails from old Juwie, the fisherman, so that we could spend the afternoon fishing for klipfish. Or we might roam further south along the coast to Lager Bay; here we once found a harpooned whale, which had been washed ashore.

'From the back stoep at Ganzekraal we had watched the whales gambolling in the bay, their enormous dark shapes clearly visible; we could even see them spouting after a dive. Two whalers had sailed into view. We could see the puff of smoke as the harpoon was fired and a little later off they went, towing the whales alongside, to the whaling station in Saldanha Bay. One of the whales had broken adrift, to the joy of the local women who bore home on their heads paraffin tins full of the vile-smelling oil smelted out of the blubber. Many whale bones – ribs, baleen and huge vertebrae – were strewn across Lager Bay beach; Father took some of the largest vertebrae home and we children used them as stools on the front stoep.

'Father regarded his wheat, rye and barley with a professional eye, and remarked to Mother that the lands were coming along nicely. We children, looking out of the other side, saw the fallow lands and the two "islands" – outcrops of stone and bush which had not been cultivated and which formed islands between the sea of wheat.'

Frances explains what became of her mother's family home. 'Long after the Melcks sold Ganzekraal, the homestead was badly burnt while owned by William Duckitt. The remains of the homestead, which were considerable, were bulldozed by a tenant farmer in 1989, I think.'

Today, nobody at the holiday resort knows about the old beach cottage or the family who lived here. They just know it's a wonderful place to put your feet up and do some great fishing.

This spread *Yzerfontein is an excellent holiday destination where you can kick off your shoes and relax. During winter, the sea is a dramatic picture made up of a brooding sky and iron-grey sea.*

Message in a bottle

Finding a bottle washed ashore, with a message inside it, is every child's dream. In 2005, when William Townshend was digging for mussels in the soft sand in the Jakkalsfontein shallows close to Yzerfontein, he came across a bottle with a note in it (*see right*). The writing was faded and, sadly, it didn't contain directions to a pirate's buried treasure but rather captured a man's musings. Who knows where he wrote the note, or how long it had been bobbing in the sea, but it found a home with a young boy who too will grow to be a man and may one day, 30 years from now, remember the message he found in a bottle.

This spread *Finding a bottle with a message in it is every young boy's dream and William Townshend was quick to compose a response to throw back into the sea.*

It's a sunny 17 July winter's day. The background roar of marbled waves merges into the rounded silence. Chuckles and the murmur of conversation lull my mind into a semi-daze, solitary, detached and included in the group. Detached like the two fishermen. Standing on the last roll of pearly white sand, drifts of conversation fade in and out, carried by the wispy sea breeze, like flipping through the stations of an all-but-turned-down radio. But secure in the fellowship like the four feet planted together in the shale, licked by the frothy wavelets, listening to but not partaking in conversation.

david

the background roar

of marbled waves

CT469

Seaweed snacks

Next time you're exploring the rock pools along the West Coast, be sure not to ignore the many different types of seaweed or sea plants growing there – many of them are packed with minerals and proteins and are great to eat. Just a few of the seaweeds you can expect to find on the coast are kelp (*Ecklonia maxima*), purple laver (*Porphyra capensis*) and *viltvingers* (*Codium fragile*).

Louie Lemmer has been researching seaweed for years and shares some of her wisdom about purple laver, which looks like bits of crinkly black plastic bag when it's dried on the rocks.

'Porphyra is best known to us as nori, the imported, pre-treated article sold in health shops for use in sushi dishes,' says Louie. 'Our South African variety, fresh off the rocks, needs a little more attention in order to release its full culinary potential, but it is well worth it, as I've never known a vegetarian who wasn't hooked after the first bite! This is probably because of the very high protein content – as high as soy beans – 100 grams of dried nori supplies one half of the daily adult protein requirement. Add the fact that the calcium content is 10 times that of cow's milk, the vitamin A content equals that of eggs or chicken livers, and that it is one of the richest sources of vitamin C and the B vitamins, including B12, not to mention the full range of trace elements, and it all makes perfect sense.' One of Louie's favourite dishes is nori fritters *(see right)*.

Nori is the easiest seaweed to collect fresh as it is exposed on the rocks at low tide. The dark green slippery sheets of seaweed dry to almost black in the sun but a mucilaginous layer prevents it from drying out completely and the plant revives with the incoming tide. Be sure to cut the seaweed leaves with a sharp knife so that you don't dislodge the foot of the plant which, Louie explains, will sprout a whole new crop.

'Once home, quickly wash in cold water,' she continues. 'But don't soak it as the precious minerals will leach out. Drop the seaweed directly into a lightly oiled heavy-bottomed pot, or leave out on a clean sheet to dry in the sun and wind. Make sure to bring it indoors at night, otherwise the dew will stop it from drying out completely.

'The dried nori lasts almost indefinitely stored in a cotton or linen pillowcase in a dry airy place. The freshly picked nori may also be kept in the refrigerator for a few days before it is rinsed and cooked. Boil over low heat, first adding a bit of lemon juice or vinegar, four tablespoons to a six-litre saucepan. This is essential for breaking down the tough structure of the plant, and to release its full flavour. Simmer until it is a mush – the consistency of oats porridge – about three hours. More water may be added during the cooking process if necessary. If you are using dried nori, cover the nori at the start of the process with water and reduce the cooking time to one and half hours. When ready, season with salt and pepper to taste and a dash of sugar if preferred. Now it is ready to be used. The cooked nori can be kept in the refrigerator for a couple of days or you can freeze it.'

Nori fritters

Heat 2 tablespoons oil and 1 tablespoon butter in a heavy-bottomed frying pan (preferably cast iron). Shape patties from the cooked nori, dip into oats and fry until nicely browned on both sides. If your mush is too runny to shape patties, spread a layer of oats into the oil of the pan, spoon a layer of nori on top, sprinkle oats over, dot with pieces of butter, fry until brown underneath, turn over and brown. For variation add fried chopped onion to the mush before making fritters.

But it's not just on the West Coast that purple laver is popular. It's eaten in vast quantities in Japan, while in Wales it is used to make laver bread, which is boiled laver mixed with oatmeal, lemon juice and seasoning and deep fried. It's usually served with bacon and eggs for breakfast and gourmands squeeze a little fresh orange juice onto the dark bread. It's also occasionally served with Welsh mutton, used to thicken soups, and in seafood stuffing.

This spread *It's hard to believe just how fast the West Coast is changing. Where once there used to be seaside shacks and old whitewashed cottages, there are now mansions that command enormous prices. This old photograph from the archives captures a vanishing way of life – a rowing boat, fishing nets and simple fishermen's cottages.*

Darling and surrounds

Throughout the centuries, Darling and the rolling hills that make up the district have always been sought-after agricultural land. Today it's an up-and-coming wine growing area.

Groote Post

Peter Pentz is a striking figure with his Kangol beret and extravagant grey goatee. Although he retired from dairying a few years ago, he's not the sort to sit around doing nothing and pretty soon took up a new challenge. He's taken to wine farming at Groote Post like the proverbial duck to water and – together with his son, Nick – is turning out world-class wines.

'My family were in the dairy business for years,' Peter explains, 'but milk is a faceless product. Nobody is going to cross the street to shake your hand and thank you for the fabulous bottle of milk they had! I was sad to sell my herd, but the lifestyle is punishing. You can never take a day off and getting up early in the morning 365 days a year is tiring.'

The farm has a long history, tightly bound with that of the Cape. Peter continues, 'It was an important refuelling stop for boats sailing between Europe and the East. In 1706 (when farmers were settling in the Riebeek Valley) Governor Willem Adriaan van der Stel granted permission for stock to be grazed at Klawer Vallei (Clover Valley) – the farm where the Groote Post was subsequently established. The cattle and sheep were intended as meat for the passing ships and to supply the hospital at the Cape where sailors were sent to recuperate from scurvy.'

The stock also served as a magnet to cattle thieves and it became clear to the Dutch East India Company that to safeguard their property, they would have to build a series of army posts or stations to keep out the marauders. As the name suggests, Groote Post was the biggest outpost in the area, just below the slopes of the Kapokberg with magnificent views across the bay to Table Mountain. Over the years, governments came and went and Groote Post changed hands a number of times. But it did serve as an important experimental farm under the watchful eye of agricultural superintendent William Duckitt in the early 19th century.

William had 10 children – the most famous of whom was Hildagonda Duckitt who went on to write two books that made her a household name: *Diary of a Cape Housekeeper* and the better-known *Hilda's Where is it?*

Hildagonda wasn't only interested in turning out the perfect batch of scones. She also collected the seeds of the pretty *balseminie* plant that she found growing in profusion on Groote Post and sent them to a nursery in England where they were identified as *Nemesia strumosa*. These flowers were hybridised and their seeds distributed around the world. The restaurant at Groote Post, Hilda's Kitchen, is crammed with old-fashioned utensils that would have been used when feeding the hordes of visitors who passed through the farm. The hearth and oven were reportedly so large that 35 loaves of bread could easily be baked at one time.

When Peter Pentz and his family bought Groote Post and Klawer Vallei in the late 1980s, the farm was run down and in dire need of attention. The photograph albums in the wine tasting room are a fantastic record of how one man's dream can transform a landscape. With the help of old Arthur Elliot photographs – taken at the turn of the 1900s when he toured the Cape taking his, now famous, black and white photographs – the Pentzes were able to rebuild the old gable that had been reduced to a pile of rubble.

Today the farm is 4 000ha, 120 of which is given over to vines. More understated, but perhaps even more valuable, is the 400ha of *renosterveld* on the farm that will remain untouched. '*Renosterveld* is disappearing at such a rapid rate,' says Peter, 'that we are determined to conserve what we have left on the farm. For now we are the farm's custodians and it's the right thing to do.

This spread *Groote Post wine farm, one of the oldest homesteads on the West Coast, has a commanding view over the bay to Table Mountain. The cool sea breeze that comes off the Atlantic has proven to be excellent for the vines and Groote Post white wines keep raking in the awards. Owner Peter Pentz is also committed to keeping as much of the endangered* renosterveld *intact as possible.*

My own happy memories of Klaver Vlei are of days in the veld, walking many miles to shoot a buck or guinea fowl. I remember the south-east wind on my face; the snorting of the horses; grilled mutton and pork chops, with a choice of sherry, brandy, red wine or beer when we met the wagon at lunch time. Jannie Kirsten, with his old-fashioned high collar and leggings and hammer-gun, divining for water with twigs of wildedagga. Martin Ruperti, our host, talking about this favourite dish – tortoise pie. The gables of the homestead glowing in the late afternoon sun as we trudge in line uphill through the heavy sand along the river bank.

Author Lawrence Green on
Klawer Vallei and Groote Post.

Kukumakranka

Johnnie Frans, together with his horse, Bles, is getting ready to ride out to check on the new lambs. He must be at least three score and ten and one eye is more than a little milky. His horse's back is dipped from years of hard work. Johnnie's dogs mill around and – although his joints might be creaky and stiff – there's little else he could imagine doing. He's been on the farm all his life and knows the curves and contours of Groote Post like the back of his weather-beaten hand.

Tucked into the band of his hat is a thin, yellow, pod-like plant. Its smell is powerful and sweet and Johnnie is thrilled at his find. It's a kukumakranka – as much a part of the West Coast landscape as *bokkoms, blomme en mense net soos hom.*

South African National Parks manages the nearby West Coast National Park and a spokesperson explains more about this unusual plant, 'One of the summer-flowering West Coast plants is the kukumakranka or koekemakranka. There are about 32 *Gethyllis* species, of which *G. afra* and *G. spiralis* are perhaps the most commonly used ones. Koekemakranka is one of the few Khoi words still in use and is an example of the contribution that the Khoi people have made to the cultural wealth of the Western Cape.

'These interesting plants all have an underground bulb of which the scales form a distinctive neck at ground level. The long, thin leaves are usually spirally twisted or coiled. The attractive flowers appear in summer when the leaves have already died. They have a narrow tube, which extends below the ground where the fruit will eventually develop. In mid-winter, the long, club-shaped berry emerges from the ground. It has a fragrant pulp in which numerous seeds are embedded. The ripe fleshy fruits are highly aromatic and have a powerful sweet, fruity odour. The gathering of the inconspicuous fruit depends to a large extent on a good sense of smell.

'Kukumakranka brandy was one of the early Cape remedies for colic and indigestion. Traditionally an alcoholic infusion or tincture was made from a few ripe fruits in a bottle of brandy or witblits. The edible fruit was also highly valued to perfume rooms and linen.'

This spread *Scenes from Groote Post. Johnnie Frans spends his day in the saddle as a shepherd of yesteryear tending to the stock and checking the fences on Groote Post. He's tucked a kukumakranka, a rare West Coast find, into his hat because the fragrance is so potent and brings back memories of days gone by when it was easier to find these plants in the veld.*

It has just rained and there's a big field mushroom nestled on some straw in the back of John Duckitt's bakkie. The mushroom is a good sign – it seems there might be rain this year after three years of a punishing drought that has wreaked havoc with wheat farming in the Western Cape.

'Ja, it's been a tough couple of years,' says John over tea and his wife Jeanette's home-made rusks. He echoes the feelings of all the farmers one speaks to.

The Duckitts are to Darling what the Cloetes are to Constantia. They're old family and have not only inherited the treasures that have been collected over the years, but also bear the weight of perpetuating the family name and fortune.

The original South African William Duckitt was brought out to the Cape as an agricultural adviser when it became clear to the authorities that Boer farming methods were outdated and would never be able to fulfil the needs of the growing population of Cape Town. After protracted preparations, William and his family arrived in Cape Town in September 1800 on a ship that could best be described as a Noah's Ark.

According to Paul Duckitt who helped prepare the booklet commemorating the family's bicentennial reunion, which was held in 2000, 'He brought a Devon bull and two cows with him that were from the prize herd of Francis Russel, the 5th Duke of Bedford, which was managed by his brother John Duckett (note the different spelling of the surname). He also had 20 half-bred Spanish & Ryeland ewes and two rams. He brought seed valued at £300, as well as hop plants, fruit trees and machinery, which included two drill ploughs designed by his father, two ploughs with Skim Coulters, three sets of harrows for difficult work, a complete set of horse shoes, a horse scuffle and a cart and wagon for husbandry use. It is thought that the hop plants may have died during the journey as no further mention is made of them.'

William started an experimental farm in the Paarl area, but progress was slow and the local farmers were wary of his new farming methods, which they deemed too expensive and impractical. He persevered, buying a shop in town to help pay the bills, as well as Paradise Farm in Newlands. It's hard to believe that Paradise Road in Newlands, which is now an increasingly congested highway, used to be part of fertile farmlands that stretched for miles.

A series of land swaps saw William move from Paradise Farm to Witteboomen in Constantia (you can still see remnants of the original farm on the road from Constantia to Hout Bay), which he didn't like at all because it was far too boggy, and then on to Klawer Vallei. It was there that he worked on improving farming methods on the experimental

This spread *An old photograph of Darling shows just how much it's developed. It may no longer be a remote rural village, but its spring flower displays are just as magnificent.*

DARLING

farm at Groote Post. At Klawer Vallei and Groote Post William Duckitt's fortunes changed. He, together with the Van Renen brothers, had the lucrative meat contract supplying the army and navy.

Paul Duckitt writes, 'William spent the remainder of his life at Klawer Valley, using most of the 2 800 acres for cattle and sheep and about one tenth for cereal farming, consisting of wheat, barley, oats and rye, with a smaller portion for grapes. He organised a racing stud, mating his mares with sires supplied mainly by his Van Renen friends. A number of his horses ran at the Green Point track, earning him a further profit from his sale of horses. He also had a blacksmith shop in Klawer Valley that was used for manufacturing harrows as well as two- and three-furrowed ploughs according to his father's designs.'

For all the impact that William Duckitt had on the Cape's agricultural landscape, it was his granddaughter Hildagonda (baptised Hillegonda) whose name has endured. She was multi-talented and very accomplished: an expert horsewoman, a talented seamstress and a respected botanist. In addition to the nemesia plants she sent back to England, she also sent over the seeds of the 'Stars of Bethlehem' and *bokbaaivygies*, which made it possible for them to be propagated and distributed around the world.

However, it was her housewife's helper, *Hilda's Where is it?* for which Hildagonda is best known. Her alphabetical recipe book is more than just that, however. In amongst her friends' and family's favourite recipes – Bessie, her mother, Mrs Kotze, Mrs Dwyer and Mrs Dan Cloete are just a few of the contributors – it contains useful household hints. Next to soufflés, for instance you're likely to find a tip on how to remove wax or semen stains out of silk! Hildagonda might never have married (more about that later) but she certainly wasn't a prude!

There are remedies to treat a variety of ailments. Horse colic, chilblains, croup, eczema and Cape distemper in dogs are just a few of the maladies that are given short shrift with a mixture of drops of laudanum, peppermint oil, whisky, *nux vomica* and anything else with healing properties that Hilda could gather from the *veld*.

Her book also gives an idea of the times she lived in, when men rode for miles each day to reach their destination and meals were made for the hungry and active. The dishes she lists for breakfast are extensive and robust and muesli and low-fat yoghurt don't even begin to get a show in!

Breakfast dishes

See Brawn, Croquettes, Chicken (Scalloped), Eggs (Curried), Eggs (Poached), Eggs (Scratched), Fried Bread, Fish, Fritters (Beef, etc), Ham Toast, Herrings, Kegeree (sic), *Kidneys, Mushrooms, Mutton Chops, Omelets* (sic), *Oysters (Scalloped), Porridge, Ragout, Rissoles, Rolls, Sausages, Scones.*

But for all Hildagonda's successes, the dark spot in her life came in the form of William Brown. The Duckitt Family Reunion booklet contains this entry; 'She met a Lieutenant William Brown to whom she became engaged. The engagement dragged on for seven long years, and when she was all packed up with her trousseau to leave for England, and staying at Groote Constantia, prior to sailing, she received a letter from her fiancé to say that money was still a great problem. If she came over he would marry her, but that any children would be brought up in squalor, all in the harshest words.

'Hilda was heartbroken, but her uncle advised her to break off the engagement at once, as nothing could be worse than a loveless marriage. William Brown in turn had other plans. He received a promotion and married a wealthy widow, who had to be admitted to a hospital for the incurably insane, where she died. Hilda was an extremely proud woman and never again referred to this incident. It was only on her deathbed when her niece was clearing away papers, letters and photographs that she admitted, "he had spoiled my life".'

Hildagonda died in 1905 after a painful illness and is buried in St Johns Cemetery in Wynberg, Cape Town.

John and Jeanette and their family, the present-day Duckitts who live at Waylands, have all this history and more to refer to. There's a cupboard in the main house that would have historians and nostalgia-lovers rubbing their hands in glee.

When the cupboard is opened, the smell hits you immediately: it's strangely medicinal and makes you want to sneeze. The collection is haphazard and at times a bit strange. There are beautiful ladies' riding crops with carved silver heads, a letter dating back to 31 May, 1825, which dealt with an inspection of the slaves on the farm, dog tags from the war and a book containing daily rain records dating from 1910. There are snuffboxes, a dusty roll of tobacco that still has a rich but fading aroma and fishing line made of twine and coated in ox-blood to strengthen it and stop it from rotting. Medals won at various agricultural shows for prize bulls and their Suffolk Punch horses are a testimony to the Duckitt's farming skills.

It's a treasure trove – a highly personal collection that offers insight into this pioneering family's life.

This spread *A trip to Darling wouldn't be complete without visiting Evita se Perron at the old station. You can't miss it – just look out for the bright pink building! While you can just pop in to enjoy* 'n lekker bord boerekos, *it certainly is worth staying for a show. Playwright Pieter-Dirk Uys remains as funny and incisive as ever as he continues to spoof prominent politicians or to take on the persona of his legendary alter ego, Tannie Evita Bezuidenhout.*

Tannie Evita

It's hard to know what Doctor Hendrik Frensch Verwoerd (former South African president and architect of apartheid) would have to say about Doctor Pieter-Dirk Uys. Well, it's not that difficult actually. He's probably turning in his grave in shock and horror that one of his own, a good *boereseun*, could behave so outrageously. Of course Pieter-Dirk and his alter ego Tannie Evita wouldn't have it any other way. Outrageous is what they do best, and now Pieter-Dirk Uys has been awarded a doctorate for his seriously funny and funnily serious work. What's more, in 2005, Evita even had a road named after her when the Moorreesburg Pad was renamed the Evita Bezuidenhout Boulevard with much fuss and fanfare.

What could be more apposite than Pieter-Dirk Uys and Evita Bezuidenhout, living in a village called Darling? He's the darling of South African satire, and his speech is peppered with dramatic and warm-hearted 'dahlings'. Tannie Evita is as much a South African icon as rugby, biltong, sunny skies and, well, politics!

But let's backtrack. Evita Bezuidenhout debuted in a newspaper column written by playwright Pieter-Dirk Uys in the 1970s. He wrote as though he was an insider of the Nationalist Party and perfectly placed to dish the dirt. His mysterious source's voice grew so strong that she was soon nicknamed the 'Evita of Pretoria'. She hit the stage in the early 1980s, when apartheid was in full swing and the ruling Nationalist Party was short on humour.

The titles of his shows and some characters are intricately bound up with South African politics and life, which partly explains why Uys has been so successful. His first production, *Adapt or Dye*, for instance, was based on a speech by former prime minister P.W. Botha, who said white South Africans must 'adapt or die'. For a country ripped apart by politics based on colour, it was a play on words Uys couldn't pass up. Every deeply layered performance shows an astute understanding of the country and her people. One of his characters, Nowell Fine, for instance, is named after the delicious and truly South African phrase 'Ja, no well, fine ...,' which is uttered before saying what really has to be said.

Over the years, just a few of his productions that have had audiences rolling in the aisles include *Farce about Uys*, *Total Onslaught*, *Skating on Thin Uys*, *A Part Hate A Part Love* and *Dekaffirnated*.

Most politicians were happy to be lampooned – in an inhumane society, laughing at themselves made them seem more human. And, if there's any criticism levelled at Uys, it's that for all his biting remarks, he played court jester to the apartheid government and pulled back when he could have gone for the kill. He would argue that shows need a balance between punches and tickles. Too many punches don't put bums on seats; too many tickles end up being vacuous.

Uys is not just about comedy and satire, however. He's deeply committed to transforming society. Before the first democratic elections in 1994, he embarked on self-funded voter-education tours. He's now channelling his considerable energy into tackling HIV/AIDS. As with his performances, he pulls no punches. During his talk he demonstrates how to put a condom on a banana. This he swiftly replaces with a life-like rubber penis, 'Because,' he explains with a twinkle, 'men and boys don't have bananas between their legs. A condom on a banana on the bedside table is not going to protect you!' Of course the kids shriek with laughter and according to him 'the black teachers turn white!'

Uys is a huge fan of Nelson Mandela, and the former president has an enormous amount of time for the satirist. On Mandela's long imprisonment Tannie Evita said, 'He's very grateful we kept him from Winnie all those years.' In 2002 Uys was nominated as a national living treasure by the South African Human Sciences Research Council and joins a group described as 'magnificently creative South Africans who have achieved excellence, critical acclaim, and international success'.

You can catch Tannie Evita at Evita se Perron in Darling. Look out for the shocking pink building, which used to be the old Darling Station before it got a new lease on life when Pieter-Dirk Uys moved to town. It's a fabulous venue cluttered with Afrikaner memorabilia. After shifting one of the resident cats off a chair, you can have a hearty meal and watch a show.

Here's to you, dahling!

***This spread** There's nothing like a painting of pincushion proteas by famous South African artist Vladimir Tretchikov to make you feel at home, and Evita se Perron is bursting at the seams with knick-knacks you'll recognise instantly as South African. Love the flocked wallpaper, dahling!*

Ja, no well, fine ...

Favourites

You can't leave the area without:

- **Stocking up on fresh olive oil** and olive products at the many farms and farmstalls in the area. Kloovenburg is a good place to start. You can do both a wine and olive tasting before selecting what you want from their wide range of tapenades, oils and body products. The Olive Boutique in Riebeek-Kasteel is also well worth a visit. Watch olive oil being pressed before sampling the different products.
- **Sipping a glass of Allesverloren Port** while relaxing next to a blazing fire at one of the many restaurants in the valley.
- **Spending a Saturday morning browsing** at the Riebeek Valley morning market that's held on the first Saturday of each month. You'll find a bit of everything to suit your magpie tastes: homemade produce, bric-a-brac and a great sense of community.
- **Enjoying a picnic** at Groote Post. Imbibe some of their fantastic wines and soak up the history of the 18th-century farm while lying on the lawn under the trees. Don't forget to order a day ahead.
- **Going to the annual Darling Wildflower Show** that usually takes place in September. The Duckitt Nurseries Orchid Show normally coincides with this event so you can enjoy a profusion of flowers.
- **Enjoying the Darling Wine Experience**. There are some outstanding cellars to visit, including Groote Post, Darling Cellars, Cloof and Ormonde. You'll find some good wines that are really reasonably priced. Brilliant for everyday enjoyment.
- **Booking for a meal and show** at Evita se Perron. Make sure you have enough time to browse through all the *boere* kitsch that clutters the venue and then sit back and enjoy one of South Africa's best-loved satirists.
- **Spending a luxurious weekend** at Bartholomeus Klip. It's a country retreat that has it all – great food, oodles of charm and beautiful surroundings. Enquire about the special themed weekends. It could be food and wine pairings, botany, or stargazing. Either way, you're in for a treat and might never want to leave.
- **Capturing the magic** of the Riebeek Valley in autumn when the vines are a burnished red and orange. Take along your paints and plenty of courage. The inspiration is all there, you just need to unlock your talent.
- **Taking a slow drive** through the village of Mamre. The old whitewashed Moravian church buildings at the centre of town are beautiful and there's a real sense of nostalgia in the place. At one point in the mid-1900s Mamre was renowned for producing excellent housekeepers who were sought after for all well-to-do Cape homes.
- **Switching off your cellphone** and having a real beach holiday in a seaside cottage. You can pump for white mussels (delicious fried in a little butter and served with a squeeze of lemon), fish off the rocks or spend hours looking in the pretty rock pools.
- **Writing a message** to put in a bottle. Getting it out beyond the surf line might be a bit of a challenge, but you could always find a friendly boat owner who is prepared to drop it into the ocean for you.
- **Looking for a dog-eared copy** of Hildagonda Duckitt's *Hilda's Where is it?* to browse through.
- **Visiting the Rondeberg Nature Reserve** on the R27. The reserve is proud of the more than 900 species found here, including rare disas you aren't likely to find elsewhere. You need to phone ahead and book a guide who can show you around and help you identify the different flowers.
- **Having a fish braai** overlooking the Atlantic Ocean. If you don't manage to catch one of your own, head down to the fish market as you come in to Yzerfontein. It's usually humming around lunchtime when the boats have landed. You'll have to compete with some seriously cheeky seagulls wheeling overhead.

Tourism Bureaux

West Coast Tourism: (022) 433-8505

Darling Tourism Bureau: (022) 492-3361 or darlinginfo@mweb.co.za

Riebeek Valley Tourism Bureau: (022) 448-1584

Yzerfontein Tourism Bureau: (022) 451-2211/366

Contact numbers

Allesverloren wine sales: (022) 461-2320

Cloof: (022) 492-2839, www.cloof.co.za

Darling Cellars: (022) 492-2276, www.darlingcellars.co.za

Darling Wildflower Show: (022) 492-3361

Duckitt Nurseries Orchid Show: (022) 492-2606

Evita se Perron: (022) 492-2851, www.evita.co.za

Groote Post – cellar and restaurant: (022) 492-2825

Kloovenburg: (022) 448-1635, www.kloovenburg.com

Olive Boutique: (022) 448-1368

Ormonde: (022) 492-3540

Rondeberg Nature Reserve: (022) 492-3099, www.rondeberg.co.za

Where to stay

Bartholomeus Klip: (022) 448-1820

Floral Cottage: (022) 448-1271 or 083 454 1258

Kasteelberg Country Inn & Bistro: (022) 448-1100

Lighthouse, Yzerfontein: (022) 451-2380 or 083 300 6869

The Travellers Rest Country Inn & Guest House: (022) 448-1383

Trinity Guest Lodge: (022) 492-3430

Waylands Guest House: (022) 492-2873 or 072 211 567

This spread *Lavender bushes stand proud outside the Vyge Vallei Farm Stall on the R27 where you can stock up with freshly baked bread and other farm stall treats. The store also has a wide selection of local art, so you could buy a painting to remember the area by.*

Sand, sea and sky

Langebaan, West Coast National Park, Churchhaven, Saldanha, Paternoster, Velddrif

It's the call of the sea that dominates the small towns that have sprung up along the West Coast – strung out like pearls in a pretty necklace. There's nothing precious about life on the coast, however. The seasons are hard and dramatic – but that's part of their charm. Who could resist the startling blue sea, acres of spring flowers and the enticing smell from a fish braai? The vast Langebaan Lagoon also keeps drawing visitors back to its aquamarine shores and sheltered coves.

Langebaan

It's a windswept day in Langebaan. When you half-close your eyes (you have to anyway because the wind is so fierce) the lagoon looks like a giant lemon meringue – whipped up, with white frothy peaks. Gulls take off but are sent scudding backwards before they find a calm spot – flapping furiously, but going nowhere.

The kite-surfer with a neon orange and pink kite isn't faced with the same problem. He's flying across the lagoon at breakneck speed, lifting off, airborne for what seems to be an eternity before hitting the surf again. At the water's edge a man and his son are busy pumping for prawns, windcheaters flapping like crazy and puffing out, making them look like smaller (but only just) versions of the Michelin man.

The Langebaan lagoon is intoxicating. Sure, the wind heaves and thumps for much of the year, but the lagoon has a charm that keeps people coming back year after year – or prevents them from ever leaving. The town has changed a lot over the last ten years. Old seaside shacks have been replaced with multi-million rand mansions, and the dirt tracks that used to criss-cross the town are now tarred. For all the changes, however, Langebaaners are proud of the town's continuing laid-back atmosphere. Their slogan is, 'Live life slow'.

'We don't have the big five,' they quip. 'We have the slow five – the tortoise, whale, sandshark, dune mole and porcupine.'

Tucked away in the side streets is evidence of the older, simpler Langebaan. There's a sweet little cottage with a generous *stoep*, corrugated iron roof, a bright blue gate and a palm tree out front. Over the road, an *oomie* in a home-knitted jersey is sitting outside, on a porch filled with African violets, enjoying the weak winter sun, while just down the road four noisy children shoot up and down on a trampoline, shrieking as they go.

Colin Meyer is a Langebaan old-timer and lives in one of the original cottages, which was built by his parents, stone by stone, around 1926. He's a *regte* Meyer *(see pg 72)* – one of the first families in the area, who have been working the lagoon for generations. His cottage is a treasure trove. On the wall hangs a huge poster portrait of Lady Di in a red dress, and a painting of a smiling naked woman reclining on the rocks looking like a mermaid surprised to be washed ashore. Tiny tortoise shells decorate the wall; they are all that remains of a crow's feast that was collected from the *veld*. Out back is an enormous water tank from the days before the town had fresh water, when residents relied on the winter runoff for their supply of fresh drinking water.

'The first road in the village was tarred in 1960. Electricity came in 1955 and fresh water the same year,' says Colin while he carries on cleaning his day's catch of harders. He goes out twice a week now for fish he dries and sells to regular customers, but there was a time when Colin only ever spent around 10 days a year on shore.

'I signed up on a whaling boat when I was 16,' he explains with obvious pride. 'I started out as a general dogsbody. You all did in those days. We made good money whaling and although it was a hard life there was lots of freedom and nobody to tell you what to do. You were your own boss and everything was free on board, so when you came ashore you were a rich man.'

Previous spread *Langebaan Lagoon in magnificence and moodiness: tranquil views towards Geelbek in the West Coast National Park; windless late spring days on the tidal reaches; another of the National Park's treasures, the birding paradise of Abrahamskraal – the perfect place to spot migrating birds; the yacht moorings at the Greek-style Club Mykonos resort just outside Langebaan.*

This spread *Abandoned boats on deserted beaches are West Coast icons. This one at Churchhaven provides a new home for algae and insects.*

there's nothing

there any more

Living
life
slow

Seb's secrets

Seb's Fishing Tackle shop in Langebaan is the fisherman's equivalent of a sweet store. It's packed with brightly coloured fishing essentials: sinkers, reels, line and a multitude of luminous lures, to mention just a few. In his shorts and slops, Seb Di Capua can't do without his daily fix of surf and fish.

'Whenever I get a *bietjie moeilik* (a little difficult), my wife hands me the keys to my boat and tells me to go fishing. It's an almost instant cure to any bad mood you might be experiencing,' he explains. 'The thing I tell people is that you should never go out to catch fish. Go out to relax and unwind. If you catch something, well, that's the bonus.'

Nobody, however, said that a passion for fishing and good sense of humour don't go hand-in-hand. Seb's boat is called *My G Spot* for all the obvious reasons. He smiles when he mentions the boat's name.

'The water has been very "pretty" this year,' he says. 'And so have the fish. We've been catching up to four different species on one day.' Of course Seb's fishing is not haphazard – and that's why people enjoy charters with him on *My G Spot*. There's a science, and an art, to catching fish that has plenty to do with sophisticated swivels, traces, hooks and other complicated gadgets. Seb has produced a guidebook and map that he sells to customers to give them an insider's view of the Langebaan Lagoon. It's not a foolproof guide to fishing, but it is a start.

It begins: 'The information supplied is merely a guideline to the lagoon fishing. Bear in mind that fishing patterns may change at any time (as per fishes' decision).'

When it comes to recommending suitable bait, his sense of humour is never far from the surface. According to Seb's Lagoon Guide and map, stumpnose, steentjie and elf all have particular dietary preferences. Stumpnose opt for prawn, white mussel, pike, pilchard and red bait. Steentjie are less discerning. For their choice of food Seb writes, 'Food is food, my man. Bring it on, anything will do.' Elf are more picky – pilchard (preferably filleted) or pike are favoured.

'The thing about fishing,' says Seb sagely, 'is that no trip is ever the same. Each trip is a new experience – and that's what I like.'

Ah, yes. In every fisherman lurks a true philosopher.

Previous spread *Langebaan's old-fashioned beach houses are fast being replaced by flashy mansions on the hill and speak of the town's changing fortune.*

Take a windswept walk along the jetty at the Langebaan Yacht Club to admire the expansive view across the sea. If the wind is howling, you'll need to watch your step!

This spread *This Langebaan fishing spot looking onto Schaapen Island has many different moods, depending on when you visit. At sunset it's a reflective place to cast a lazy line or two. Poles from an old jetty provide an ideal perch for watching gulls.*

Global village

The tidal mudflats of the Langebaan Lagoon serve as a summer stop-over for thousands of migratory birds each year. While some of the birds might be hard to identify when they're on the move, their names certainly stand out. Look for the delicate greenshanks with their spindly yellow legs, or the frenetic little stints that dart around in search of food. Less common, and therefore even more exciting to spot, is the bar-tailed godwit with its delicate long bill.

Since the late 1960s, the Western Cape Wader Study Group has been ringing the large numbers of curlew sandpipers that touch down in the national park each year. However, a great fluctuation in the number of first-year birds – ranging from plentiful in some years to extremely scarce in others – confused the group.

It turns out that birds breeding in the Taimyr Peninsula in the far north of Russia, 13 000km from Langebaan, are affected by just how well the lemming population is doing. In years when there are no lemmings, the curlew sandpiper population takes a sharp dip as sandpiper eggs and chicks fall prey to the Arctic foxes that usually feed on the small rodents.

West Coast Fossil Park

The science is there to explain how bone, shell and teeth are transmogrified to stone but, for all our understanding and research, it still seems magical. There is, quite simply, something astonishing about being able to touch a fragment of life from over 10 million years ago, and it's the process of fossilisation that makes it possible.

A visit to the West Coast Fossil Park just outside Langebaan on the Langebaanweg Road is a riveting experience. One of the richest sites in the world, this brings you face-to-face with timeless wonders as you survey the ancient relics from the late Miocene and early Pliocene epoch.

Who knows if the fossils would ever have been uncovered if it hadn't been for the CHEMFOS Ltd phosphate mining that took place on Varswater farm. It started with the discovery in 1958 of an elephant tooth and the anklebone of a short-necked giraffe. After it became clear that the quarries being mined for phosphate were even richer in fossils, mining ceased in 1993 and 14ha of abundant deposits within a 700-ha area was declared a National Monument. Today the West Coast Fossil Park is a public private partnership between BHP Billiton mining company and Iziko Museums of Cape Town.

Although it's hard to believe, a mere (in palaeontologist's terms) five million years ago Langebaan was a lush, forested area, which was home to a number of animals that are now extinct.

Pippa Haarhoff, the manager of the West Coast Fossil Park, explains about the digs that are currently underway. 'The dominant animal being excavated in what was an ancient river channel is the giraffid *Sivatherium hendeyi*, which was one of the most common large herbivores inhabiting this region five million years ago. The *sivatheres* is only one of over two hundred species so far discovered at this site.'

Other animal remains that have been found include the elephant-like *gomphotheres,* the sabre-toothed cat, and sea mammals such as whales, dolphins and seals. However, the dominant predator living in this region in those far-off times was the African Bear, *Agriotherium africanum*. The remains of at least 11 specimens have been collected and this animal has been adopted as the logo of the Fossil Park.

In his book, *Langebaanweg – A Record of Past Life*, Q.B. Hendey provides more interesting information about the African Bear. He writes, '*Agriotherium* was an enormous animal, as large as the living Kodiak bear, an animal that may reach a weight of 750kg. By contrast, lions generally weigh up to 200kg. *Agriotherium* is also unusual in having been a largely or exclusively carnivorous bear, a characteristic shared by only one living species, the polar bear. This is curious since the closest living relative of the *Agriotherium* is the giant panda of China, which is the most herbivorous of the living species.'

According to Hendey, the giant panda is threatened with extinction in the wild partly because of its specialised diet – a fate that also befell *Agriotherium* several million years ago. 'This ancient animal could no longer find sufficient food to feed itself in the rapidly changing world of the Pliocene.'

The West Coast Fossil Park is committed to making the past as accessible as possible. One of the old mine offices has been converted into a visitors' centre, where regular lectures are held, and there are exhibits of some of the fossils found at the site. There are digs the general public can participate in, and new cycle trails and hiking routes have been established. Better still there's a great tearoom attached to the centre. Where else could you get a Sabre-wich, a Gompho burger or a Bear breakfast?

How are fossils formed?

- Impregnation: when dissolved salts slowly impregnate buried bones, teeth, wood or shells.
- Mummification: when a 'body' is trapped in an enclosed oxygen-poor space, preventing it from decomposing completely; organisms trapped in amber are also fossilised in a similar way.
- Substitution: when bone is lying in soil or rock, over centuries the minerals, such as calcite or silica, seep into the tiny spaces within the bone, so helping to harden and fossilise it.

This spread *The West Coast Fossil Park is a national treasure and contains one of the richest reserves of fossils from the late Miocene and early Pliocene eras. Regular tours are conducted when you can get up close and personal with bones dating back centuries, and sift through trays of small fossils for valuable finds. The jaw bone shown belongs to* Sivatherium hendeyi, *a short-necked, long-horned giraffe.*

a whale roar can be heard kilometres away

Giants of the deep

It's estimated that our whale-watching industry is now worth over R490 million per annum; each year people flock to the West Coast to admire the sight of a shiny black fin or tail flip-flopping out of the clear, cold water. But the whales lolling in the calm waters of Saldanha Bay didn't always have it so good. Between 1911 and 1967, whalers in the area were responsible for killing almost 40 000 whales.

Dr Peter Best, Extraordinary Professor at the Mammal Research Institute, University of Pretoria, is based at the Iziko South African Museum in Cape Town and has been studying whales for over four decades. 'Looking across Saldanha Bay from Langebaan, one can see buildings at Donkergat and the adjacent Salamander Bay that today houses 4 Special Forces Regiment of the SANDF. Thirty-eight years ago some of these buildings were the site of one of the major industrial activities in Saldanha Bay,' he explains.

This spread *During winter and early spring you might be lucky enough to catch sight of a Southern right whale in the Langebaan Lagoon when they return to the West Coast seas to calve each year. Whale numbers have grown significantly in recent years.*

Norwegians went on to dominate the development of modern whaling and the first land station in South Africa was opened by Johan Bryde and J.J. Egeland in 1908. The following year Bryde obtained permission to build a land station at Donkergat, but this was only completed in time for the 1910 season. However, this delay didn't put the brakes on whaling off the West Coat as Bryde operated an old sailing barque as a floating factory in the bay. The flensed carcasses of whales were towed out to sea and dumped. Not everyone was happy with this ad hoc arrangement: the practice resulted in complaints not only from passing sailors about 'dangers to navigation', but also from farmers in North Bay, who claimed the stench from decomposing bodies put the flocks off their grazing!

'Bryde was soon in deeper trouble,' Dr Best goes on to explain. 'Despite giving an undertaking that he would not trade with a country at war with

the UK, in December 1914 he sold some whale oil and meal to Germany. As a result he lost his licence in 1916 and Irvin and Johnson took over the station. Johan Bryde's name lives on in a species of whale, Bryde's whale, first described from his land station at Donkergat and Durban.'

The Salamander Bay station too had strong Scandinavian connections, with the buildings being dismantled in Iceland, transported to South Africa and re-erected in Saldanha Bay. The manager, Hans Ellefsen, donated many of the whale skeletons now in the South African Museum. In the years between 1911 and 1930 the two stations made a significant dent in the whale population and processed 17 500 whales, including at least 6 400 blue whales, some up to 95ft (29m) in length. After the 1930 season both stations closed, Salamander permanently.

Although the Donkergat station was re-opened for three further periods, whaling finally came to a halt in 1967 because the whale stocks were so severely depleted by over-fishing.

'Now whales are beginning to reappear in the vicinity of Saldanha Bay,' continues Peter. 'Between May 2002 and February 2003, Mammal Research Institute observers at North Head spotted 375 humpback, 705 right and even two blue whales. It seems clear that the international protection efforts, begun as long ago as 1935 by a League of Nations agreement, are now paying off.'

Southern right whale (*Eubalaena australis*) is the whale you're mostly like to spot in these waters. The whale's name says it all – this was the 'right' whale to hunt because it was rich in oil and baleen and floated when killed, making it easy for the whalers to retrieve. It was so ideal, in fact, that it would have been hunted to extinction if it hadn't been for the international treaty that came into effect in 1935, providing it with protection.

Every *Weskusser* needs some handy whale facts to impress visitors:

- Southern right whales can measure up to 15m and may weigh 36 tonnes;
- Most of them spend the summer months down south, feeding in the icy waters of the Antarctic before heading up to warmer waters to mate, calve and raise their young;
- Females return every third year between the end of May and early July to give birth to a single calf after a gestation period of about a year;
- To sound like a crusty old sea salt you need to be able to tell your humpback from your Southern right. You can recognise the Southern right by the wart-like callosities on the head, squarish flippers and lack of a back fin; humpbacks have a dorsal fin, long wing-like flippers and no head callosities.

Whale terms

- Breaching: leaping from the water in an arching back flip. Every time a whale breaches it uses up the same amount of energy a human uses in two days.
- Grunting: a whale roar that can be heard kilometres away.
- Lobtailing: slapping the tail flukes on the surface.
- Spyhopping: standing vertically with head and body as far as the flipper above the surface. This allows the whale to get a clear view of its surroundings.

West Coast National Park

It's the colour of the Langebaan Lagoon that first grabs your attention; it's azure, aqua, sapphire and cerulean, although the palette changes in a second according to the seasons, the time of day and the mood of the weather.

The lagoon is the focal point of the West Coast National Park, which stretches from Yzerfontein in the south, to Postberg up north and takes a wide sweep inland until it abuts the R27. In spring the Park's beauty is most obvious, with the *veld* strewn with multi-coloured flowers that tumble down towards the white sands and blue, blue sea. But the salt marshes that make up so much of the lagoon's edge have their own, albeit more subtle, appeal. Their colours are muted greens, reds and grey – a tone poem much like a piece of music by Edvard Grieg or Richard Strauss.

But the West Coast National Park and the lagoon are not just good for looking at and hoping that your happy snaps will do them justice. They are also significant in terms of the number of migrating birds that stop off there and for the fossils that have been found in the vicinity.

***This spread** Sunsets on this west-facing coast are legendary and you'll experience plenty of dramatic moments while visiting the Langebaan Lagoon and the West Coast National Park. The Park explodes in a riot of colour each spring when the wild flowers bloom, but sightings of the wide variety of birds that use the lagoon as a migratory stop-over are just as noteworthy. The Park's cottage at Abrahamskraal, a stone's throw from the water's edge, is for rent.*

The Langebaan Lagoon is an internationally acclaimed and recognised Ramsar (Wetlands Convention) Site, and home to hundreds of different species of birds that feed off its bounty. Birders will be quick to tell you of the astonishing sight of thousands of greater and lesser flamingos standing in the shallow waters. But it's not just the flamingos that attract attention; the Park is also home to the largest breeding colony of black harriers in the world and, at last count, Malgas Island at the mouth to the lagoon boasted around 70 000 breeding pairs of Cape gannet.

When you tire of birds (as if there's any likelihood of that happening!) you can keep an eye out for some of the other animals that roam the Park. These include gemsbok, red hartebees, bontebok, springbok, eland, mountain zebra, wildebeest, Cape and bat-eared foxes and African wildcat. The threatened angulate tortoise is another Park resident and you need to keep your eyes peeled when you're driving as they're inclined to wander onto the warm tarmac – going nowhere slowly.

Postberg Nature Reserve, on the northern arm of the lagoon, is nothing short of a national treasure, with its overnight hike a particular favourite. Although within the West Coast National Park, it is only open from August to September – just in time for the spring flowering season and the whales. Catch a glimpse of these behemoths from Tsaarsbank or Plankiesbaai where they swim so close to shore it feels as though you can step off the rocks and onto their shiny backs.

Geelbek

Elmarie Leonard is the driving force behind Geelbek Restaurant, which is situated at the southern end of the lagoon. Geelbek serves delicious food, and acts as a convenient visitors' information centre. The restaurant is located in the homestead of the original farm and the low-slung, whitewashed building with its unpretentious gable presides over the lagoon with a quiet solidity. For years Elmarie has been scouring the local communities for recipes. A descendant of Angela of Bengal, one of the first freed slaves in the Colony, she finds the mix of cultures, traditions and food absolutely fascinating.

While investigating the culinary traditions of the different nationalities that influenced the local food, Elmarie also did a great deal of historical research and she explains the significant role Geelbek played during the early days of the Colony.

'The homestead was built in 1761 and looked much the same as Geelbek today. It served as an important water stop for travellers journeying up the coast. The trek from the Castle in Cape Town took over 32 hours to the Oudepos fort at Kraalbaai and was a hard slog over sandy dunes through uncharted territory.'

According to Spaarman, an expert *karwyder*, an ox wagon travelled at 4km per hour. In 1732 the ox wagon dirt track was frequently used by travellers from Cape Town who stopped at Groene Cloof, which is where Mamre is today, Geelbeksfontein and then at De Bottelarij before they headed north to St Helena Bay. Unfortunately, the original farmhouse was burnt down in 1781 by the postmaster Mnr Stofberg to prevent its takeover by foreign troops. It was rebuilt in 1860 by Alexander van Breda.

'In 1785 the VOC beacon was planted at Geelbek to mark the most northerly border of the Dutch East India Company (Verenigde Oostindische Compagnie). You can still see the beacon today on your way to the bird hide. The name of the farm probably comes from the yellowbill duck that you see in the area rather than the geelbek fish,' Elmarie continues.

'In 1920 Geelbek was the largest wine cellar in the country – not because grapes were grown in the area, but rather because the Governor General, Henry de Villiers Steytler, used Geelbek to store his vast amounts of wine. He also dredged the lagoon to allow ships to shore and held many parties at his beautiful homestead. Because it was fairly remote and he was an excellent host the parties tended to last for weeks rather than just a few hours!'

True to the Governor General's *gasvryheid*, Geelbek Restaurant is always packed. Elmarie's charm and the team's excellent cooking have plenty to do with the place's popularity. Some of her favourite dishes *(see pg 70)* reflect the traditions of the West Coast. Elmarie explains that her fish roe recipe probably originated with the Norwegian whalers who worked at Donkergat before it closed down. In Norway, there's a similar recipe.

Previous spread *It's no surprise that the West Coast National Park attracts hundreds of artists. During spring the palette is a riot of white, yellow and orange, which provides a dramatic contrast to the icy blue sea. The views from Seeberg viewing point near the northern gate are breathtaking and you'll find it hard to believe you're just over an hour from Cape Town.*

This spread *It's easy to find examples of nature's art in wilder places. As the tide retreats in the Langebaan Lagoon, the sand leaves a textured pattern and offers some unusual surprises – making it a photographer's paradise.*

Sprinkle wi

coa

Stuffed harders or mullet

6 gutted harders (remove the bones with tweezers)
250g grated green pepper
125g grated onion
250g breadcrumbs
125g Cheddar cheese
125g feta cheese
salt and black pepper to taste
12 strips of rindless bacon

Season the harders inside. Mix together green pepper, onion, breadcrumbs, Cheddar and feta. Season and stuff each mullet. Wrap 2 bacon strips around each mullet to cover the cavity. Braai for 15–20 minutes, making sure your braai fire isn't too hot, or bake in a pan in the oven at 180°C for 15–20 minutes. Serve with fresh wild rosemary bread.

This spread *Harders are a real West Coast speciality and if you find stuffed bokkoms on the menu at the historic Geelbek Restaurant situated in the West Coast National Park, don't hesitate to order this dish. You won't be disappointed!*

West Coast caviar

4–6 snoek roe pockets
coarse salt
a little beer
1 egg
500ml cake flour mixed with lemon pepper
oil to pan fry

Wash the roe. Sprinkle with coarse salt and let stand for a while. Mix the beer with the egg. Dip the roe in the egg mixture then dust lightly with flour. Fry until golden brown. Serve with tomato and onion *smoor*.

th

rse salt

Churchhaven

To call yourself a true resident of the unbelievably picturesque settlement of Churchhaven you have to be a Meyer *(see pg 54)*, a Lloyd or a Barsby. These and one or two other surnames that carry weight, such as Smuts and De Nicker, are to be found in the old graveyard behind St Peter's Church. Any of the others don't count one hundred percent. Not really.

Today it's one of those glorious, wind-free days when the lagoon is a million different blues and greens, and the orange, white and yellow spring flowers are beginning to show their faces. Standing on the steps of the whitewashed church, with its green painted steps and bright red geraniums in pots, you could have stepped into a travel brochure. There's a bell tower, inscribed '1905', in the corner of the churchyard and a view over the lagoon that you would be hard-pressed to match.

And it's this little slice of paradise that the locals so fiercely want to protect. There are big Private Property signs posted at the entrance to the settlement. Drive down the badly eroded path and somebody is bound to wave you away while pointing at the Keep Out signs. These are people who have lived in relative isolation for years and who want to protect their privacy.

Eben Meyer (yes, he's part of the Churchhaven nobility) is busy packing plastic chairs and tables into the back of his *bakkie*. It was Aunty Joey's 90th birthday party the previous evening in what used to be the school hall and everybody contributed tables and chairs for the occasion. Eben grew up here and, in between lugging chairs around, says simply, 'It's far better than paradise.'

This spread *The pretty but tumbledown graveyard at Churchhaven has one of the best views over the Langegaan Lagoon and is the final resting place of early settlers in the area. Look out for common family names such as Lloyd, Barsby and Meyer.*

Local lore has it that the very first residents were pirates who sheltered on the calm shores of the lagoon before heading out past Schaapen Island and through the mouth of the lagoon to rob unsuspecting vessels.

At the beginning of the 1900s, the settlement threw off any whiff of skulduggery and built St Peter's Church overlooking the sea. It was part of the parish of Malmesbury and, according to the notice pinned to the church door, one of three mission stations on the shores of Saldanha Bay. The other two were Langebaan and Hoedjiesbaai.

The church was consecrated in 1905 and the Archbishop of the time wrote of the community that had worked so hard to build the church: 'they had already contributed £83 in money, and at least £150 in labour and material, and £44 was still needed to clear off the debt. But the people had determined to do this on the day of dedication; and they did it. The collection was £53, of which over £40 was given by the fisher-folk themselves. You should have heard the cheers outside the little church when the amount of the collection was announced after the service. The catechist tells that no case of drunkenness or immorality has been known in the place for more than ten years.'

How a few private families ended up having homes in the Park is interesting. Until the 1980s, privately owned land abutted the lagoon. But, when it became clear that this area was rich in natural resources and worthy of preservation, government conservation bodies stepped in.

Negotiations with residents began well before the 1988 demarcation. The then Parks Board, now SANParks, made a deal with the descendants of families who had been living in the area since the mid-1800s. They agreed to keep their cottages and the small strip of land along the lagoon edge and, in the interests of conservation, contracted to sell the rest of the farm from the lagoon in the east to the mighty Atlantic.

The farm was Stofbergsfontein, named after the postmaster at Postberg during the days of the Verenigde Oostindische Compagnie (VOC), more commonly known as the Dutch East India Company.

Churchhaven is named after the little church with the astonishing view over the lagoon. Residents don't refer to their settlement by that name. That's too general for them and they live either in Pottebakkery, Bossieskraal or Schrywershoek. This would be an excellent place to hole up and write, if only you could find a cottage to rent for a few months. They're rarer than hen's teeth – booked out years in advance by the same families who come to holiday here. However, life on these shores is simple. There's no electricity, no running water and no popping down to the local café for a loaf of bread or an emergency chocolate.

'After 10 days you need to get back to town to have a proper bath,' comments one holidaymaker who isn't a Meyer, a Lloyd or a Barsby.

'There used to be two shops,' says Eben. 'The school was built in 1938 and it went up to Std 5 (now Grade 7), which in those days was referred to as a *boerematri*ek. Nobody studied further than that. You were needed on the farm and didn't need to know much more than the basics. As a child I remember hunting in the *veld* and my parents tell stories of sitting around the table waiting for my grandfather to shoot a buck for supper. But now a lot of the older people don't live here permanently any more; they have passed away or they've moved to town.'

Although home ownership is fiercely protected, there's nothing to stop residents selling to uitlanders. Property prices have rocketed – not surprisingly because everybody wants a slice of paradise.

'It makes me very heartsore when people sell up,' laments Eben. 'Things are changing. It used to be a very tight-knit community, but not so much any longer.'

Many changes indeed. People living here used to work at the Donkergat whaling station or survive from the sea. The whaling station closed decades ago and now it's really difficult to get fishing permits. Luckily, despite shifts and reforms, some things remain the same. Don't be tempted to make the mistake of trespassing. Nothing about that rule has altered!

Nevertheless, you can also experience a piece of this heaven at Kraalbaai, which is open to the public. Heading in a northerly direction, you will find this lovely sheltered bay just down the road from Churchhaven. The water is blue and calm, the sand white and you can find a spot next to a rock and spend your day dozing, messing about in the water or just basking in the sun.

Saldanha

Just 13km south of Vredenburg, Saldanha is situated at the northern corner of one of the biggest bays and is a water enthusiast's dream. It's hardly surprising that every man and his boat heads there for the summer hols, where they spend their days in costumes or wetsuits strapping on their water-skis and firing up their speedboats for a morning's fun on the glinting water.

Saldanha's fortunes have waxed and waned over the centuries, but it's now associated with the milling and shipping of steel and iron-ore. The town was named after Admiral Antonio de Saldanha who was wounded on these shores in 1503 by a group of Khoikhoi while taking in supplies. A century later, in the early 1600s, Saldanha Bay rivalled Table Bay as a potential safe harbour for ships traversing the seas, and it was only the lack of drinking water that prevented it from becoming a major port along the southern tip of Africa.

The town didn't always have a reputation as a good holiday destination. For about a decade at around 1870, the then-isolated bay also served as a quarantine station when a ship carrying people with a contagious disease had to be removed from Cape Town as fast as possible. Smallpox sufferers were regularly banished to this far-flung place and the graveyard at Salamander is the final resting place of many who didn't pull through.

It's suggested that Doc's Cave is named after a medical doctor who lived in the cave at the time of the quarantine. He is thought to have treated patients, who arrived but were prohibited from setting foot on land, in small dinghies!

Today, the town has shaken off any traces of its gloomy past and people head to Saldanha for a different type of healing that only holidays at the beach afford. There are relaxed seafood restaurants near the water's edge and you'll be able to feast on fresh catches of crayfish, fish, mussels and oysters. The Hoedjieskoppie Nature Reserve is good to visit during spring and the naval base lends a sense of purpose to the town.

This spread *Doringbaai, St Helena Bay, Stompneusbaai and Paternoster all provide plenty of wide open beaches for a solitary walk with ample time to reflect. Leaving only your footprints behind is part of the magic.*

Following spread *Although yields have declined dramatically over the years due to overfishing, Saldanha Bay still provides a substantial catch for these fishermen who are used to rising well before daybreak for a full day on the waves. When the snoek are running, there's no holding them back and no disguising their joy.*

Paternoster

Everyone in the area seems to be called Boeta. There's a staffie with little road sense being called to safety: '*Kom*, Boeta!' In the space of a morning two vehicles, with number plates marked Boeta-At WP and Boeta-2 WP, flash past. Etched into the old white wall outside Die Winkel op Paternoster, Boeta has staked his claim by writing 'Boeta for Pearl' in rough, uneven lettering. Maybe there's something in the fertile soil that fosters the robust types who make up these small towns. These are 'okes' who smoke pipes with cherry tobacco, crack open beers far too early in the morning when other people are having tea and rusks and say, '*Donner*', '*Bliksem*!' and '*Die blerrie* government' quite a lot.

Of course that's a generalisation, but towns are often caricatures of themselves. That's what's makes them so interesting to visit. Furthermore, not everyone fits the mould and that makes the experience all the richer.

Paternoster is a picturesque little fishing village hunkered down on the windswept coast. The drive there is both remarkable, or not, in that contradictory West Coast sort of way. When the wheat fields are winter green, or the light from the setting sun is burnished and golden, it's lovely. But, at the end of summer, the landscape has a hard, breathless edge to it, which makes travellers desperate to see the blue of the sea.

Paternoster means 'Our Father' and there's speculation that the village got its name from the prayers sent up by desperate Portuguese sailors shipwrecked on the rugged rocky shore. Today, it could well be for the prayers and curses sent out by frustrated fishermen who weren't granted fishing permits and are stuck at home watching the shoals of fish swim by.

Permit troubles, or not, every year hundreds of holiday makers with fishing and diving on their minds head for this stretch of coast to camp and caravan at Tietiesbaai in the Cape Columbine Nature Reserve which, during springtime, lights up with a thousand wild flowers. It's not a sophisticated holiday destination, and chances are visitors will go to sleep with a fair amount of sand in their camp beds each night. But it's blissful and when everybody's *skottels* are hot and the smell of bacon and eggs wafts over the campsite, plenty of Tietiesbaai fans wouldn't be anywhere else in the world.

This spread *Die Winkel op Paternoster is one of the town's original buildings and gives an idea of what the fishing hamlet would have been like in olden days. Treasures from the sea decorate the Paternoster se Padstal.*

Old men of the sea

Fishing quotas regularly make the newspaper headlines. While everyone acknowledges fish stocks need to be conserved and allocated more equitably, for many men who grew up in boats and had sea legs before they could walk on dry land, the changes are hard to stomach. One such man is John Murray. He grew up in Paternoster and his *ouma* used to live in the house that is now the Voorstrandt restaurant, right on the beach.

'Paternoster existed because of the fishermen, but that's all changing and people are doing a good job killing it off,' says John from his house perched on top of the rise with a spectacular view over the bay. The wind is pushing and the sea is too rough to go out, but even if he wanted to, he couldn't. It's that damned permit issue again.

'These days the young men can't follow their fathers out to sea. Now they have to look for construction work or go to Saldanha. When I was 12, I learnt how to make fishing nets from my father. I'm in my 50s now and have fished all my life. Now that I don't have a permit, I can't do what I know best. When the harders are running, I can't sleep I get so excited. The sea is in my blood and you can't escape from that.

'I don't understand it. *Die vis is nie skaars nie* (the fish are not scarce). I can stand on my *stoep* and you can see the shoals coming across the bay. They jump out of the water there are so many of them, but I'm denied the right to make a living. There are times when there's nothing in the house to eat. Nothing. Just R2 in my wallet. Now there are all these regulations – who can use a trek net, who will get a hand-line permit and what fish you're allowed to catch. What they don't seem to realise is that sometimes it's the snoek running and other times it's something else. They can't tell you that you can only take out one kind of fish. It makes no sense – you need to fish a little from many different kinds and they all come together to provide a decent living. But I'm still lucky in a way because my sons got permits and our community stands together.

'People can't imagine it now, but we used to fish without cellphones,' says John with a laugh. 'I don't have one, but everybody else does so they just phone to find out where the fish are running. I remember we used to have somebody sitting in the dunes, and they would light a fire when they saw a shoal of fish moving across the bay. That way we would know to get our boats out. Or else they would take off their shirts and run around like mad men. '

And, as if the permit story isn't enough, John has another story.

'Ah,' he says with a shake of his head. 'I don't remember all the details. Ask Johnny back at the hotel, but in the 1960s government officials came to our house and asked us if we wanted to be classified *blankes of nie blankes nie* (white or non-white). My *oupa* had three wives, and one of them was white, so some kids were dark and some were light. At the time our neighbours decided to be white, but my father couldn't have been bothered so we're classified coloured.'

Crazy world. Only in South Africa.

This spread *The Paternoster se Padstal stocks a range of fabulous jams and seafood delicacies, which you can taste before you buy. One of their best sellers is the pickled octopus or 'tjoka', which is delicious eaten cold by itself or served in a salad with chunky wholewheat bread.*

Jan Visser, Paternoster artist

The old Sandveld names to look out for around Paternoster, Velddrif and beyond are Coetzee, Smit, Brand, Kotzé, Visser and Lambrecht. These were the first *boer* families to trek into the harsh interior of the West Coast to eke a living from the sandy soil.

It seems appropriate somehow that Paternoster artist, Jan Visser, one of these pioneer descendants, lived until recently on what used to be a farm called *Pelgrimsrust* (Pilgrim's Rest). He's on his own kind of pilgrimage: journeying to a place of beauty and truth through his art. He rises at three, much as his farmer forefathers would have done, and starts painting by four o'clock, well before the sun rises and touches the lip of the hill where he built his studio overlooking the sea. Jan came to be a full-time artist only at the age of 37 after losing enthusiasm for his law practice.

Though he is best known for his nude studies, his landscapes are breathtaking. They're neither pretty nor comfortable. They're striking, demanding of your attention, and insist that you look – and then look again. He has managed, by some magic with his pastels and oils and textured paper, to capture the magnificence of the West Coast scenery. It's no small feat. How do you begin to capture the space, the wind, the colours and the textures of the rolling fields?

One of his paintings shows familiar wheat fields cut through the middle by a huge *donga*. The gaping hole is filled with delicate pen and ink drawings of a mishmash of skulls, old wheels, fishing tackle – the detritus of human existence.

'I love the space you find in the West Coast,' says Jan simply, 'but there is a sense of foreboding about the land. It's also so interesting. When you first look at the landscape you think that nothing is going on, but I watch the *veld* from my studio and veranda and there's so much activity.'

Jan has a drawing that captures the essence of the Sandveld – planes of fields, each textured with the lines made by a plough just before the winter rains. It's a landscape that anybody who has driven through the area will identify with immediately.

'Ja, so much for all this fancy land art that people are doing these days,' he says with a quiet smile. 'These *boere* boys from the area knew all about it long before it became fashionable to arrange poles, stones and things out in the open.'

This spread *The pristine Groot Paternoster Nature Reserve is just around the corner from Britannia Bay and the perfect spot for sundowners. Artist Jan Visser is a man of the West Coast – enthralled by the rugged landscape and sparse beauty, which he captures in many of his striking paintings.*

Voorstrandt restaurant

Hedwig van der Westhuizen owns the Voorstrandt restaurant right on the beach. On a blustery winter's day she's wearing gorgeous patterned stockings and a pinkish furry woollen overcoat that makes her look a little like a friendly yak. She's an ex-Capetonian who in the early 1990s gave up the bright lights of the city for a 10ha smallholding in the middle of nowhere near Vredenburg. After the crush of the Mother City, the vast spaces and sparseness of the West Coast took some getting used to but Hedwig soon found her feet when she opened the Voorstrandt restaurant, a Paternoster institution.

'Paternoster is lovely and one of the things that give it character is that the community is integrated. It was never really that affected by the Group Areas Act, which tore most of South Africa apart.'

How this happened is one of those anomalies that pepper South African history. Originally there were three farms – Gaatjie, Kraaifontein and Vaalplaas – which all intersected at a point where the village developed. Coloured fishing folk mostly made up the communities but, because they didn't own the land or the cottages they were living in, the government wasn't able to force them to leave. And so the village stayed, and has continued to grow. Now it's developing at a phenomenal rate, which has its pros and cons. In the 1994 elections there were around 555 registered voters. The voting tied between the National Party and the ANC so they drew lots and the National Party won.

'The thing about small towns,' continues Hedwig with a twinkle in her eye, 'is that at some point everybody is cross with each other and nobody will talk to you. It's the nature of small town politics. But arguments soon blow over and there is a real sense of belonging, which is wonderful. And it's very social. On Tuesday night we partied until about three in the morning.'

On a Tuesday?

'Why not? Life along the coast is hard,' says Hedwig. 'The mainstream commercial fishing industry is very unromantic and we don't get a huge variety of fish. If there's a snoek run, then you salt it, smoke it, and eat snoek until it comes out of your ears. Of course there's always mussels and crayfish during season.

'Poaching is a problem. Not just here but all along the coast. There's a great story of a local poacher who occasionally will ask people to look after his dogs for the morning, otherwise they follow him down to the sea where they wait patiently for him. All the flora and fauna guys (known more formally as Marine and Coastal Management) have to do is look out for his dogs to catch him red-handed when he comes out the water.'

Hedwig's mild seafood curry is famous but she's also proud of her kelp pickle *(see right)* – a real West Coast favourite for special occasions.

Veld food

The West Coast landscape might look sandy and barren, but for generations people have been collecting food from the veld. The understanding of what is or isn't nutritious is passed down through families from father to son or mother to daughter. Unfortunately, as more people move to the city, this history is lost.

Maria Pieterse grew up in the Calvinia area, but has been living in Vredenburg for the last 12 years. She works at the Weskus Spens (a home produce store) just outside Vredenburg on the way to Paternoster. She's a child of

This spread *The view towards Paternoster from Groot Paternoster Nature Reserve.*

edible but slimy

the *veld* and grew up on a farm. During the holidays Maria and her siblings accompanied their dad who was a shepherd and lived out in the veld for long stretches of time. 'It was a lovely way to grow up and we learnt from my dad what we could eat from the veld.'

Top of Maria's list is the brightly coloured *botterblom* or gazania (*Gazania krebsiana*). They flower during spring and summer and transform drab tracts of land into fields of gold. 'When you chew them,' Maria explains, 'they are very creamy which is why they're known as *botterblom* or butter flower. You don't cook the flower – you just pick it and eat it.'

Next up is *pietsnot,* which sounds a lot less appealing, although it is also known as yellow satin flower or *Grielum humifusum*. The fleshy, protein-rich roots are edible, but slimy, which accounts for the name. The plants are eaten fresh as a source of moisture in Namaqualand and are favoured by duikers.

Suring (sorrel or *Oxalis*), which produces both pink and yellow flowers, can be eaten raw and is an important ingredient of *waterblommetjiebredie*. The leaves can be used to flavour potato dishes. It's got a sharp, sour-ish taste, which makes your cheeks suck in but is also quite compelling. However, too much of it is not good for you and *Oxalis* poisoning is not unheard of in sheep.

A treat for anybody scanning the *veld* is *veldkool, hottentotskool* or *bokkool* (*Trachyandra falcate*). These delicate spears, which don't look that different from asparagus shoots, are delicious cooked with lamb or other fatty meat dishes. 'You can also eat them by themselves. All you need to do is boil them lightly. The flavour is delicate and delicious.

'When I eat *kos* from the *veld*, it reminds me of my childhood,' she reflects a little wistfully.

Kelp pickle

Collect kelp a day after it's washed up. Trim off the leafy bits and use the top 30cm of the tube. Wash out any sand that may be inside – a small bottlebrush helps. Peel with a veggie peeler and cut into 1cm rings. Soak in iced water overnight. Boil in water until soft – about 15 minutes. Drain, return to a clean pan and add the pickle mixture. Simmer for 10 minutes and bottle hot. Leave it to pickle for 2–3 days and once open, store it in the fridge. It tastes great with pâté and home-made bread and is delicious sliced thin and served with sushi.

Pickle mixture (enough for approx 4 cups sliced kelp)

1 cup grape vinegar
¾ cup water
¼ cup sugar
1 teaspoon black peppercorns
1 stick cinnamon
1 tablespoon soya sauce

Velddrif and surrounds

Wind down the car window and take a deep breath! You're near Velddrif where the river and sea converge and there's nothing to beat the smell of soft briny sea air, foggy mornings and the salt marshes. It's the smell that speaks of beach holidays, early mornings spent puttering up and down the river in your boat, and late afternoon *braais*.

The name of the town dates back to earlier days when cattle herders moved their animals up and down the coast in search of the best grazing. A favourite spot was the *veld* near the ford or *drif* across the Berg River and it wasn't long before the area was referred to as the '*drif* in the *veld*' or Velddrif. However, it wasn't cattle farming that drew people to the area – it was the rich harvest from the sea and in the 1940s factories sprang up to process the pilchards, snoek and harders that were pulled from the icy ocean.

This spread *A boat lies abandoned on the Berg River while Hannie and Sakkie Thaart and the family dog soak up the warm early morning sun on the stoep of their cottage close to the river's edge.*

It's also worth remembering that this rich stretch of coast has attracted people for centuries. The Khoekhoen fish traps and shell middens that are scattered along the coastline are a reminder of our *strandloper* ancestors who roamed the shore. Other explorers included Portuguese navigator Vasco da Gama, who opened the trade route between Europe and India. In November 1497, Da Gama and his crew anchored near the Berg River. They spent eight days restoring sails, scrubbing down the ships and stocking up on supplies before setting sail again.

Remember the song, '*Daar kom die Alibama, die Alibama die kom oor die see* ...'? One of the stories goes that the little sailing cutter, the *Alibama* made many trips up and down the Berg River. She also made the journey to Table Bay loaded with *dakriet* (the thatching reed of the Sandveld) and *matjiesgoed*, for tying the bundles of reed. One particular type of river reed was used in the making of bedsteads for Cape Malay brides. Custom had it that wedding guests would feast on Malay cuisine, view the 'Alibama bed' covered in white and silver bedspreads and a Malay choir would sing a folksong in honour of the little cutter, '*Daar kom die Alibama* ...'

Harders: a West Coast cash crop

Fishing for harders is not new. As early as the 17th century, Dutch settlers were using beach-seines or *treknets* to catch the shoals of fish that moved through Table Bay. The catch they were after is the southern mullet (*Liza richardsonii*), which makes up the harder or *bokkom* industry on the West Coast. According to an ichthyologist, the southern mullet is the most abundant of the 15 species found in our seas and is endemic to our waters. Harders grow quickly and can reach around 20cm in three years.

The biggest problem with the harder industry is what's known as 'bycatch'. Nets are notoriously unselective and the term refers to fish that are caught incidentally. Concern was raised as early as the 1960s when a commission of inquiry was set up to establish which species of line fish were being depleted due to net fishing.

Marine and Coastal Management explains: 'In the Western Cape, St Joseph sharks comprise about 25 percent of the bycatch. Other species that are commonly caught in harder nets are yellowtail, white *steenbras*, *elf* (shad), grunter and *galjoen*.'

The price difference between what you can get for harders and line fish is an inducement to fishermen to target more expensive, but out of bounds, species. What is very sobering is that of the 40 or so line fish species that are caught, at least 18 are endangered and adult populations are down by around 25 percent.

Another problem, and you only have to hang around fishermen for a short period to understand that it's a real one, is the under-reporting of what is being caught. Permit holders are compelled to submit details, but in many cases catches and especially bycatches are drastically under-reported. In some incidences, it's not malicious. These are mostly not 'nine-to-five' men fond of filling in forms. They get up before first light, ride the waves and the wind, and come back with little desire to fill in documents. There is, of course, also a degree of rebellion. These men with scarred hands, who have had hooks through their eyebrows or who first put out to sea when they were nine years old, don't like being told what to do. Their fathers didn't fill in forms, so why should they?

Bokkoms

Gut and wash the harders thoroughly. It's not necessary to scale them. Salt the fish very well with coarse salt and layer them in a large container in a cool place overnight. Next day remove the fish from the salt and thread a length of strong twine through the heads of around 10 fish. Hang out to dry in a windy place. Remember to bring them in at nightfall as moisture will rot the fish. Depending on conditions, it will take about eight days for the fish to dry thoroughly.

This spread *The* bokkom *or harder industry plays an integral part in the West Coast economy and drying racks line the bank of the Berg River where you can buy a batch to take home with you. A young* Weskusser *is proud to show off his early morning catch.*

serious stealth machines

Barn owls: stealth killers

Take a drive down a Velddrif back road that cuts through the expansive fields of grain and you're likely to spot what look like large postboxes mounted on high poles. The mystery of these is solved when you meet farmer Quartus Laubscher who has been living and farming in the area his entire life.

'They're barn owl nests or boxes aimed at encouraging these birds back onto the farms so they can help keep the rodent population at bay,' explains Quartus on his grain farm, Cloeteskraal.

'The gerbils eat everything,' he goes on. 'They dig holes in the ground and then when we plant the seeds for the lupins we graze our sheep on, they go crazy.' In the past Quartus has spent up to R40 000 a year on pesticides to kill the rodents before they destroyed his crops. His farm, like many in the area, is enormous at 2 000ha and expensive to manage.

'The other problem is that there were so many gerbil holes that it was impossible to target each one individually,' he goes on to explain. 'As a result we were forced to sow poison pellets everywhere. But, as you can imagine, this is very damaging to the environment and every year lots of birds are killed unnecessarily.'

Quartus is a *boer* and every *boer* always makes a plan. He decided to introduce barn owls to his farm, as they have done in other countries, as a more effective way to control the gerbils.

'But barn owls need barns,' laughs Quartus, 'and so I got building. But you've got to be sure to build a box with an opening just big enough for the barn owl, otherwise other birds will take them as their own.

'I'm fortunate in that my neighbour has put up owl boxes and so have a few other people in the area so our owls have a large territory to move over. We probably have around 100 pairs at the moment and this year we didn't have to put down one pellet of poison. They pick off the gerbils with ease.'

This spread *A lone gull takes flight over a calm sea. The West Coast offers some of the best birding in South Africa and there are a number of listed Important Bird Areas (IBA) within an easy drive of each other. One of the most sought-after sightings is of the threatened black-harrier.*

Barn owls (*Tyto alba*) often choose old barns, lofts and church steeples as their nesting sites. The species name *'alba'* refers to the owl's ghostly white appearance and its other names – Ghost Owl, Hobgoblin or Hobby Owl, Silver Owl, Scritch Owl, Screech Owl and Delicate Owl – reflect some of its characteristics.

But, no matter what name you choose, barn owls are very efficient killers, equipped with specially designed wings that make them serious stealth machines. A velvety pile on the surface of the feathers muffles sound. The silent flight isn't just good for catching the victim by surprise – it also aids the owl's hearing. The ear openings are at slightly different levels on the head, set at different angles and covered by a flexible ruff, made up of short, densely webbed feathers, that frames the face, acting much like a dish-type sound reflector, allowing the bird to locate prey in total darkness.

The good news is that owls have a voracious appetite. A single family of two adults and six young can consume more than 1 000 rodents during a typical three-month nesting period.

West Coast flora

The indigenous vegetation is adapted to survive punishing conditions: hot, dry and windy summers and poor, mineral-deprived, sand soil.

Renosterveld is found both in the coastal plains or lowlands as well as the mountains and is dominated by the dark, scrubby renosterbos or *Elytropappus rhinocerotis*. Renosterbos tends to grow in richer soils and in the past supported large herds of game such as black rhino, buffalo, elephant, eland, zebra, lion and cheetah. Because it occurs on more fertile soils, a lot of renosterveld has been lost to agriculture. It is also very susceptible to fire and is the most endangered vegetation type in the Cape Floral Kingdom.

Strandveld, or beach vegetation, mainly occurs on the coast that hugs the Atlantic Ocean and grows in sandy, well-drained and lime-rich soils. This plant community is made up largely of succulents, bulbed geophytes, annuals that transform the landscape each year and Cape Reeds or Restios.

Search and rescue

While rescuing plants from extinction doesn't have the high drama of elephant capture and release, it's no less significant in ecological terms. Much of the Strandveld vegetation *(see previous page)* is threatened by urbanisation, and large tracts of indigenous flora have been lost to potato and grain farming. In some instances, we may have lost species that we didn't even know existed.

Freylinia visseri, the honey bell bush or *suurlat* – a Strandveld endemic of the Velddrif area – is classified as threatened in the Red Data Book (a series of books that contain information on the threatened species of an area). This species might have been extinct if it hadn't been for the efforts of Floors Visser. Trevor Adams, horticulturist, from Kirstenbosch Botanical Garden explains how the quiet drama unfolded: 'In 1947 Floors Visser first collected a flowering specimen of this plant, which was known locally as *suurlat* or sour rod, at Hermanuskraal in the Velddrif district. He sent the specimen to Professor Compton, at the Compton Herbarium at Kirstenbosch, who recognised it as an undescribed species of *Freylinia*.

'Then in the early 1950s the owner of a farm in the Hermanuskraal area enlarged his wheat field and in the process destroyed that whole population. Mr Visser, who realised the rarity of this species, quickly collected four of the ploughed-up plants and planted them in his garden at Grootklipfontein in Aurora where only two survived.'

Years later in the 1980s when the search was on for specimens of *suurlat*, local botanists scoured the Hermanskraal area, but came up empty handed. These experts eventually managed to track down Floors Visser on his farm in Aurora. It was realised that if he hadn't saved the flora in 1954 and replanted them, the species might have become extinct. His actions were acknowledged in the naming of the plant.

So what's the fuss?

'*Freylinia visseri* is a very attractive and unusual, evergreen shrub that grows to a height of around three metres,' Trevor explains. 'The foliage adds to the attractiveness of this plant, as the leaves are oblong, firm and pointed. The beautiful tubular, bell-shaped flowers are borne in glossy dark purple clusters from September to November and during this flowering period it'll attract sunbirds to your garden.'

This spread *There are many bird hides scattered along the spectacular Berg River Estuary and in the West Coast National Park where you'll easily be able to spend a morning ticking off a myriad birds from your list.*

West Coast Bird Club

Members of the West Coast Bird Club regard themselves as some of the luckiest birders around. After all, the West Coast is the southernmost point for the Palaearctic migratory birds from northern Europe and Siberia, so they see birds most of us just dream of. What's more, they live within an easy drive of a number of listed Important Bird Areas (IBAs), a major plus in any birder's book. These include the West Coast National Park, the Saldanha Islands, Dassen Island, the Lower Berg River Wetlands, Verlorenvlei, Bird Island and the Olifants River Estuary, according to *The Important Bird Areas of Southern Africa*, edited by Keith Barnes, published by Birdlife SA (1998).

Lucille Byrnes, founder member of the club and current editor of its newsletter, *The Familiar Chat*, lives in St Helena Bay and has been bird-watching for nearly 30 years.

'The Berg River spills out at Laaiplek, and the estuary supports a wide variety of birds,' she says. One of the most sought-after sightings is of the black harrier. 'Man's predation on its breeding and foraging terrain has reduced the globally threatened endemic black harrier's numbers to less than 60 pairs in the Western Cape, five of which are known to breed in the West Coast National Park. This species is a familiar sight as it quarters along the Park's boundary fence in search of small mammals, and the athletic mating display is spectacular.

'Another plus is the sight of thousands – over 24 000 have been counted – of Cape and whitebreasted cormorants heading up river in the evening to roost on the commercial saltpans. Here too the vibrant colours of the lesser flamingos at the Carinus Bridge are also caught in the sun's setting rays. It's magical!'

It might seem like just a small detail, but one has to ask: how do you count 24 000 cormorants?

'Carefully,' says Lucille with a twinkle in her eye.

But it's not just the birds that have Lucille hopping with excitement. 'This coastline is home to a cetacean not found anywhere else in the world. Quite a claim, eh?'

Confined to the coastal waters of Namibia and South Africa's West Coast, Heaviside's dolphin, known also as the Benguela or South African dolphin (*Cephalorhynchus heavisidii*), is one of the least-known dolphins. They are classified as Data Deficient by the IUCN Red List and it is believed that about 100 dolphins a year are killed in fishing nets, further endangering this already rare species.

Learning to count

Tallying 24 000 birds sounds like an overwhelming impossibility, but for Keith and Rena Harrison from Vredenburg, it's easy. Keith explains, 'You need to find the flight path they use to the roost and sit there for the last two hours of light and count in tens as they fly past. For large numbers you need one person to record and another to count. Some birds are more predictable than others and this makes them easier to count. Cape cormorants, for example, all fly following the river over the water so their route is pretty established. But the whitebreasted cormorants are lazy and take short cuts. The Berg River lot, for instance, cut out a large bend by going across a salt marsh before rejoining the Cape cormorants past our counting point and going on to the roost.'

This is the first time that regular monthly counts have been carried out on a species from the Berg River and Keith and Rena fell into the job by accident. A proposed trip into the salt pan to monitor a tern roost proved too wet and dangerous and so, as an alternative, they went to watch the sunset by the river and started counting the Cape cormorants.

'The Lower Berg River Wetlands is an Important Bird Area (IBA) and hopefully will be declared a Ramsar Site, so information about what makes it tick is urgently needed. We are trying to get people interested in doing counts on the large signature birds where binoculars and field guides are not necessary. The problem is that observations have to be on a regular basis over several years to have meaning and aren't that glamorous!'

Keith goes on to explain that counting is a part of 'para-ornithology', where amateurs assist the professionals by gathering data from the field while still continuing to enjoy their pastime. 'Instead of the information being hidden away in cupboards, it is collated and available to help plan conservation, building, road, and tourist projects,' says Keith. 'It has taken us to areas where we would never have thought of going, and given us access to places where the public is not usually allowed. We have met some very interesting people, and of course seen beautiful West Coast sunsets and scenery.

'There are many memorable sights: lesser flamingos on a perfect evening with low sun, looking like dancing flames, or greater flamingos at full moon with the flashing red on their wings, or finding a sandwich tern amongst 850 Antarctic terns.'

Salt of the earth

Life without salt would be pretty bland. We use expressions like 'salt of the earth', and toss it over our shoulders for good luck but then just *gooi* it onto our food without further thought. Our ancestors were far more salt savvy and realised how important it was. Roman soldiers were paid an allowance to buy salt and from that wage, called *salarium argentums* or 'salt money', comes the term 'salary'. Trade routes were set up and wars were fought over this valuable commodity. The city of Jericho was founded 10 000 years ago as a salt trading city. More recently the Erie Canal was built across New York State to ship it, and the city of Syracuse, also in New York State, was funded by money raised through the salt trade.

Before refrigeration was widespread, the most common means of preserving food was through salting it, as drawing water out of food stops bacteria thriving, and so the food could be kept for years. It seems salt was also used for more gruesome purposes. In medieval times criminals were drawn, quartered and decapitated. Their heads, before being displayed on a spike in a public space to act as a deterrent to other miscreants, were parboiled in heavy brine so that they would last longer.

The tide is changing, though, and there's a growing awareness of just how important salt is. The Velddrif Salt Works produces a range of gourmet salts, including a wide range of flavoured salts that are combined with local seaweeds and herbs to help bring out the best in food. It's a combination of elements that makes this area perfect for salt production. The winds are strong and unpolluted, there are months of hot dry weather and the icy Atlantic provides an endless supply of salty water.

Britt Geach, a member of the family that founded the Velddrif Salt Works, is a firm believer that the ocean brine, which is pumped onto the salt pans and left to evaporate, contains the precious minerals our bodies need to function properly.

She explains that the first crystals to form are known as *Fleur de Sel* or 'flower of salt' and these are harvested every day. These crystals are also referred to as 'caviar of the sea' and enjoyed by gourmands around the world.

This spread *An aerial view of the Berg River salt pans near Velddrif.*

The bell at Velddrif

Gabriel Athiros, editor of *The Cape Odyssey* newspaper, spends a lot of time sourcing old stories for his publication. This is one about the mysterious Velddrif bell, not long after the Second World War.

'When South Africa was called to arms, more men from the West Coast went to fight than from any other area in the country,' he explains. 'The region was economically depressed, and there was also a strong sense of national pride which meant they signed up faster than in other areas. But when they returned from the front the West Coast was still really poor and communities struggled to make ends meet. In the early 1950s, because times were so hard, a government grocery truck travelled round to the small towns in the area dispensing food aid – sugar, flour, eggs, farm produce and condensed milk to hungry *Weskussers*.

'The course of the Berg River was also different then; the mouth didn't lead straight out to the sea and it was a lot more treacherous for boats trying to navigate up the winding channel. And when the West Coast mist rolls in, as it often does in the early mornings, visibility is very poor. To help ships find their way, the Port Captain purchased a bell, which was hung in a heavy wooden frame near the river mouth. When visibility was bad, somebody was stationed at the bell and had to ring it regularly.

'One morning a young Velddrif boy ran down to the river mouth only to find a whale and her calf beached in the shallow water. Given how poor and hungry they were, all he could think was – food! But he was worried that the whale would find a way out before he returned with men from the village so he tied the long rope of the bell around her tail, figuring that even if she wanted to move, the weight of the enormous bell and heavy wooden frame would stop her from doing so.

'That done, the youngster hared off to find his parents and call for help. But, when they returned to the river mouth, the whale, the calf and the bell were gone. The bell was found a few days later washed up in St Helena Bay. Because the bell was so heavy, transporting it back to Velddrif was a problem so they left the bell where they found it and returned to fetch it a couple of days later. Only the bell had disappeared once more!

'Now nobody knows what happened to the bell, but a few years ago it reappeared again and is now at the Velddrif Waterfront,' Gabriel finishes.

This spread *Rosy, early morning light catches the pretty stone cottages at Groot Paternoster Nature Reserve. The quaint fishing village of Paternoster lies in the distance across the bay.*

Favourites

You can't leave the area without:

- **Settling down in the bird hide** overlooking the salt marshes near Geelbek, one of the richest birding areas in the Western Cape. The best time for bird watching is early morning with an incoming tide, or late afternoon with an incoming tide, except the setting sun might get in your eyes. Look out for groups of perfect pink flamingos reflected in the water, or pelicans standing in the shallows.
- **Trying your hand at one of the many water sports** on offer in Langebaan. There's kayaking for the less adventurous or kite-surfing for adrenalin junkies.
- **Biting into slivers of *bokkoms*** on warm white bread slathered in butter and apricot jam. It sounds like a strange combination but the saltiness combined with the fruity sweetness is almost addictive. A mug of hot tea washes it down really well. Or an ice-cold beer.
- **Spending a lazy summer's day on the beach** at Kraalbaai, just around the corner from Churchhaven. Better still, hire a houseboat at Kraalbaai for a couple of days and you can wake up to the true blue of the lagoon and go to sleep at night to the sound of lapping water. Take along plenty of good books to read.
- **Explore the West Coast National Park on foot** by doing one of the overnight hikes. The best time is in spring when the flowers are out and the whales are lolling in the bay.
- **Going on a fishing expedition** with a local charter company. You can shoot the breeze with these old men of the sea who have been on the water since they were 10 years old or younger.
- **Visiting the West Coast Fossil Park**. The visitors' centre has fossil displays, and there are walking and cycling routes through the park. Phone ahead to find out if they're running any workshops or guided tours, which will give you some hands-on experience.
- **Setting up camp** at Tietiesbaai for the holidays. Take along your *skottel,* flip-flops and diving gear. This is part of Cape Columbine Nature Reserve and the marine life is still unspoilt. If you don't feel like doing it all yourself you can always stay at The Beach Camp, a tented camp just metres from the sea, run by the irrepressible Hannes. It's the kind of place where regular guests end up as friends working behind the bar!
- **Sampling the range of cured mussels** for sale at the Paternoster se Padstal. This shop, which looks much like a seaside shack, stocks some great '*Smulgoed vir die Spens*' including curried and pickled mussels and interesting home-made jams.
- **Joining a local bird watching group** on one of their bird counts.
- **Taking a boat trip down the Berg River**. Depending on the season, the colours of the salt marshes are spectacular, and the birding is always good.
- **Spending a morning at the Rocherpan Nature Reserve.** It's just 25km from Velddrif and the combination of land, sea and vlei means it's home to an enormous number of birds and is a really important breeding and moulting site. A total of 180 species has been recorded here, 70 of which are waterbirds.
- **Taking a slow drive through the West Coast National Park.** Watch out for tortoises! Stop for lunch at the ever-popular Geelbek Restaurant and hope that their *bokkoms* special is on the menu. Better still, take your bikes out and cycle through the park. If you get there early you might only have to share the road with an ostrich or two.
- **Renting a cottage at Churchhaven** for a few days. They're tough to come by but once you're there, you'll understand exactly why. When you're sitting on the *stoep* in the fading evening light, keep in mind that pirates once took shelter here.
- **Cheering on contestants in the Berg River Canoe Marathon** that takes place each winter. Find a good spot along the river, take along some rusks and plenty of hot chocolate to keep you warm while you watch them splash past in a flurry.

Tourism Bureaux

Langebaan Tourism: (022) 772-1515

Paternoster Tourism: (022) 715-1142

Saldanha Tourism: (022) 714-2088

Velddrif Tourism: (022) 783-1821

Contact numbers

Berg River Boat Trips: 082 951 0447

Cape Sport Centre: (022) 772-1114, www.capesport.co.za

Geelbek Restaurant: (022) 772-2134, www.geelbek.com

Paternoster se Padstal: 073 476 6859

Pelican Harbour Charters: 083 225 4292

Rocherpan Nature Reserve: (022) 931-2900/7

Schaafsma Chartering: (022) 714-4235, www.sailboats.co.za

Seb Di Capua Charters and Fishing Tackle Shop: (022) 772-2828

West Coast Bird Club: (022) 713-3026

West Coast Fossil Park: (022) 766-1606, www.wcfpiziko.org.za

West Coast National Park: (022) 772-2144, www.sanparks.org

Where to stay

Dolphin B&B, Stompneus Bay: (022) 742-1944, www.dolphinza.com

The Beach Camp: 082 926 2267, www.ratrace.co.za

The Farmhouse Hotel: (022) 772-2062, www.thefarmhouselangebaan.co.za

Friday Island: (022) 772-2506, www.fridayisland.co.za

Hoekie Guest House Paternoster: (022) 752-2077, www.paternoster-guesthouse.co.za

Langebaan House Boats: (021) 689-9718 or 083 269 3449, www.houseboat.cjb.net

The Oystercatcher's Haven, Paternoster: (022) 752-2193, www.oystercatchershaven.com

Villa Verano Langebaan: (022) 772-2884, www.villaverano.co.za

This spread *A perfect West Coast seascape.*

Harvest fields

Goedverwacht, Wittewater, Aurora, Piketberg, Hopefield, Porterville

If you long for country living and a different pace of life, heading inland holds some of the answers. The sense of space is both welcoming and daunting, and there are countless dusty roads to follow. You'll pass creaking windmills, drive through a waving sea of wheat and barley, and head up mountains on spectacular passes with views that last forever. These criss-crossing roads will also lead you to quaint towns packed with unusual personalities. Stick around long enough and, chances are, they will open their hearts to you and make it difficult to leave.

Goedverwacht

It's a misty morning on the N7. The dampness moves across the landscape in skeins – sometimes thickening, sometimes thinning to reveal a farmhouse bathed in early morning sunlight, or a yellow field of canola. And then it closes in again and the woolly flocks of sheep breathe out puffs of vapour and the grasses on the side of the road droop heavy with moisture.

The sign to Goedverwacht is easy to miss when the mist has closed in, but turn around if you've overshot the mark. South Africa's gems are often to be found on quiet back roads, and Goedverwacht is no exception. About 15 minutes out of Piketberg on the R399 to Velddrif, it is announced simply by an understated sign at the town's turn-off. You could be forgiven for driving by in your hurry to get to the coast, around 60km away, but you would be missing out on a real treat if you did.

Goedverwacht takes its name from the Dutch 'High Expectations' and the town has an interesting past. The farm was originally owned by Hendrik Schalk Burger who bought a slave, Maniesa, and two of her children at the slave market in Cape Town. When it became clear to Burger that the slave trade was about to come to an end, as it did in 1834, he asked Maniesa and her family to stay on the farm and look after him until his death.

In his will he bequeathed the farm to his former slave and her descendants with instructions that they should sell the farm and divide the proceeds when they no longer wanted to live there. Burger's children were less than happy with this arrangement and opposed their father's will. A court case ensued and ended up being tried at the British Queen's Council, one of the first South African cases to be contested there!

Despite his children's best efforts, Burger's will was upheld and the farm remained in Maniesa's family until her last daughter, Hester, died. You can see her grave in the Goedverwacht graveyard. Instead of selling the land on open auction, however, the family sold the land to the Moravian Mission in 1888 for £750.

Previous spread *Delicate suring flowers, loved by children for their cheek-sucking sourness, pepper the side of the road on the way to Aurora. Each season has its own charm and every view reflected here paints a colourful canvas.*

This spread *The old stone church at Goedverwacht dominates the tiny settlement and comes alive on Sunday mornings when the gospel band strikes up and the community packs the white benches for the service. Their voices soar over the hamlet's productive fields and glorious roadside flowers that bloom each year. Sunflowers, hollyhocks, daisies, gousblom and vygies are just some of the flowers proud to put on a colourful spring display.*

At the time the Moravian Church had a series of very successful mission stations at Elim, Wittewater, Wupperthal, Genadendal and Mamre, and all these settlements were bound by a very strong sense of community and religion – which is what makes them so special even in the present day.

Until the 1960s, Goedverwacht's 'Klowers' – as residents call themselves after the Afrikaans *kloof* or ravine – used to walk over the mountain to Piketberg armed with sacks of fruit and vegetables, which they would then exchange for groceries and clothes. Unfortunately this tradition came to an end when more people bought cars and transport was more readily available.

The Sunday church service in Goedverwacht is a community affair. Before the sermon begins, you can hear the band giving it all they've got. Strains of electric guitar and drums waft out of the doors that have been flung open to let in the sunshine, and down the muddy streets past the bright bougainvillea bushes, to greet parishioners making their way up to the big yellow stone church on the hill. There's a simple bunch of proteas and *fynbos* at the church entrance. They were probably picked that morning from the mountains surrounding the town and the flowers stand out against the unadorned white walls and seem all the proof you might ever need of God's glory.

The reading for today is from Matthew 11, but preaching is kept to a minimum and it's the singing that dominates. The band continues to belt out devotional songs while the congregation files in, shaking hands with whomever they end up sitting next to. There's a wooden partition running down the centre of the church, but now it's more historical than practical. During the heyday of the Moravian Church, men and women used to be strictly segregated. Today families and friends sit together and the atmosphere is much more relaxed. Surprisingly, or maybe not, the *predikant* is a woman. She's wearing a neat black hat and has fervour in her heart and a tissue in hand for her occasional tears.

A few rows ahead there's a woman with a bright red velvet hat with a gorgeous satin ribbon adorning some tight grey curls. And directly in front is a little girl accompanying her *ouma* to church. Her neat brown plaits are clamped in place with a series of clips covered in butterflies and tiny angels made out of sparkly fabric. The angels also have plaits, only theirs are a shocking yellow! The *kleindogter* has a daisy pattern bag containing R2 for the collection plate and a sweet wrapped in crinkly paper that she takes out to look at every so often. By about half way through the service, she can't wait any longer and the sweet paper gets wrinkled off and the sweet popped in her mouth.

Today's hymns seem remarkably appropriate and have strong agrarian messages. There are verses about sowing good seed, reaping what you sow and eagles soaring in the heavens. Outside in the fields just below the church, other community members are tending the neat rows of cabbages and other winter vegetables. The older people at Goedverwacht know everything there is to know about sowing and reaping and being dependent on a good crop. The younger people probably less so. There's more money to be made in town, where the living is harder and much faster.

There's a back road out of Goedverwacht that leads up the mountain towards the back of Piket-Bo-Berg. It meanders past a few derelict cottages, through somebody's smallholding (*Maak die hek toe ass.*) where you'll come out on the farm Klein Begin. As you climb up the mountain and look back over the village with its coils of smoke rising lazily and only the sound of the sunbirds going crazy on the proteas, it's hard to imagine why you would ever want to leave.

This spread *A young girl, dressed in her Sunday best, proudly displays her well-thumbed Bible outside the Goedverwacht church. Although the community is changing, the church still plays an important role in the village. Flowers, fragrant home bakes and brightly coloured washing all contribute to making Goedverwacht picturesque and well worth visiting.*

Wittewater

Wittewater or White Water is named after the waterfall that gushes behind the town after the heavy winter rains and, as with the nearby Goedverwacht, the town is a former Moravian Mission Station. By all accounts Wittewater is older than Goedverwacht and was established in 1857. It appears that the Moravians began their work in this area and only later moved to Goedverwacht when they were sold a large tract of land there.

But times are hard in the village and getting harder. The mud and thatch cottages are picturesque but the walls are crumbling and the roofs leak interminably. Jobs in the area are scarce and most of the older people do seasonal work on nearby farms – picking fruit or harvesting potatoes. It's backbreaking work that makes people look old before their time, and earns them a pittance.

Auntie Trina Scholtz is one of the town's oldest residents. She has had 10 children and lives in the house in which she grew up. The walls inside are a shocking pink while the door is a gorgeous blue. Auntie Trina, formally christened Katarina, is tiny, a frail bird of a woman with high cheekbones and her hair tucked under her scarf. But she's the matriarch of the family. There's a wedding photo of her and her husband in the lounge; her grandchildren, still dressed in their pyjamas, are drinking tea near the blackened Dover stove in the kitchen.

And it's in this tiny kitchen where Auntie Trina really wields her power. The walls are a warm yellow, the *misvloer* is packed hard from over 300 years of use, and the seat in front of the stove is shiny black and hard and looks as though it's made out of steel even though it's only hard-baked mud. The kids skedaddle when *ouma* comes into the kitchen even though the stove is nice and warm and it's the perfect place to sit and sip their sugary tea.

There's an old-fashioned iron heating up on the stove and two enormous silver pots. Auntie Trina makes fantastic bread in the oven, but it's her pumpkin fritters that are hard to beat. The recipe is so simple, she says, that she really thinks it's stupid to write it down.

Pumpkin fritters

2 cups mashed, cooked pumpkin (any kind will do)
1 egg
5 tablespoons self-raising flour
a little salt
quite a bit of sugar (about ½ a cup)

You mix all this together, shape the fritters and then fry them in some oil until brown on both sides. Sprinkle them with sugar and cinnamon while they're hot and serve straightaway.

Stoute seuns met ketties in die hand Kom om die rus te verstoor in voëltjiesland

Joyce Johannes is one of Wittewater's movers and shakers. She's a retired nursing sister and it's not difficult to imagine her in a crisp white uniform calling the shots at the local hospital.

'Now I do the Lord's work,' says Joyce. 'I get unusual instructions. One morning I woke up at three and knew I had to write a poem about Wittewater. So I woke up my husband and made him write it all down. We were finished by 12 minutes past three and everything rhymed. The Lord also told me that this poem should be decorated with flowers and framed and that every house in Wittewater should have one.

'But,' she says with regret, 'it's really costly.

'I regularly get the feeling that the Lord is telling me to do something, so now I just listen. I might get the message, "Start with the word horizon" and then everything flows from there.'

Joyce has a sheaf of poems (that one day she is hoping to publish) and formidable energy. She and her family live in what used to be the old parsonage, a sweet house and one of the smartest in town. It's got an old attic, with stairs leading up from the kitchen, filled with odds and ends. Bits of old computer, and boxes of who knows what, but not long ago it would have been filled with homegrown onions, sweet potatoes and enormous pumpkins. Like everyone else, Joyce is sad that times have changed.

O Wittewater by Joyce Johannes

God's verlate lê jy in 'n kom
Omring deur seders van 'n hoë ouderdom
Heimwee en verlange van die ou dae
Laat 'n mens soms baie vrae vra
Bo in die kloof se bloekombos
Voer die voëltjies hul kleintjies met stukkies kos
Stoute seuns met ketties in die hand
Kom om die rus te verstoor in voëltjiesland
Wyd lê die Weskus in groen gewaad
Waar dou of hael geen merk kon laat
Op die randtjies en bulte wei die bokkapaters
Om hul dors te les in die Bergrivier se waters

This spread *A woman takes a moment to sit quietly in the peaceful church at Goedverwacht. Its interior is Spartan, but its simplicity makes it even more of a haven for worshippers.* **Following spread** *Neon vygies put on a brilliant display when the sun coaxes them out. A back road from Velddrif to Aurora is transformed by a carpet of flowers, while Hillary Morris' white guava jelly glimmers like burnished amber in front of her old-fashioned Dover stove, which occupies pride of place in her kitchen.*

HEK

DEFY
DOVER

Aurora

The *dominee* in Aurora has a milk box at the bottom of his driveway. His Victorian house is perched at the top of a hill and has a great view over lots of West Coast space, and the milk box is a way away, right at the bottom of the hill at the start of the driveway. Certainly it's far enough away for somebody to walk past and nick whatever is inside it, but Aurora is the kind of village where you can leave things out and they'll be there when you come back. You can't be naïve, of course, but it still has a real small town charm about it that has long been lost in the cities. It's so safe, in fact, that there is no police station or police presence in Aurora, and little more than 600 residents.

The village is nestled at the foot of the western side of the Piketberg and its name means 'dawn light' – perfectly fitting for a place where you want to get up with first light and start your day doing whatever it is that keeps you busy. No alarm clock is needed – the birdsong is loud enough to raise the dead. For Hillary Morris, ex-Black Sash activist, it was the ideal place to escape from a hectic city life of politics and take time to make the white guava jelly she loves so much; and do the jigsaw puzzles that keep her occupied for hours at a stretch. It's also good for her godchild, Benji, who comes to stay regularly and revels in country living.

'Children can't ride their bikes in the city streets any longer,' says Hillary with concern, 'but in Aurora you can leave them playing for hours by themselves. And if they get lost, all they have to do is tell any passerby whom they are staying with, and they will be directed home.'

While all small towns face the crushing effects of unemployment and poverty, there's a sense of optimism and purpose here. The Aurora Women's Network is made up of around 15 local women who are raising funds by producing home-made paper from shredded municipal reports, using rooibos tea to colour the paper; and holding a variety of wildly popular concerts each year. The noise generated at last year's *opskop* was just about frenzied enough to scare away the many birds that you'll find in the area! There's also a soap-making project in the pipeline, and plans to develop a small caravan park that the town is hoping will attract more

tourists. The church fête is another occasion not to be missed. After the opening prayer it's a free-for-all as everybody makes a wild gladiator-like dash for the best *tuisgebakte* produce.

Oom Basie Jantjies isn't waiting for any women's network to get him going. He's been making the most amazing wooden models of tractors and wagons for decades. A master of ingenuity, he scours his environment for anything of use. His tiny workshop is packed with everything he might need to make perfect replicas of green and gold John Deere tractors. Ouma Marlie's gorgeous smile is all the encouragement he needs.

Evelyn Lombard was a machinist for 18 years at Rex Truform's factory in Cape Town. She's now set up her sewing business in an old bus that's not going anywhere: the seats have been removed and shelving installed to hold her many machines. She can make anything you want in record time, and is proudly self-employed. Hanging in the bus is the notice: *Let wel – Moenie vriendskap en besigheid meng nie.* (Take note – Don't mix friendship with business). Indeed.

One of the stranger aspects of Aurora is the stone marker on the farm Klipfontein just out of town that commemorates the arrival, in 1752, of the Abbé de la Caille who was sent from France to establish the shape of the earth. By means of some very complicated calculations he came up with a startling result – the earth was pear shaped! It was only in 1838 that his calculations were corrected by Sir Thomas Maclear, who took into account the magnetic effect the mountains would have on any readings.

Today you might think you could lose your bearings in Aurora, but it is more likely that you will lose your *lus* for city life.

This spread *Oom Basie Jantjies is a master at turning scrap into model tractors and aeroplanes. All he needs for inspiration is his wife, Marlie, whose laughter is infectious. Evelyn Lombard's dog keeps an eye on passers-by; Eva Smith tends her neat garden in Aurora.*

Following spread *Cubes of sugared watermelon glisten in a big bowl. The tannies in small towns such as Aurora produce some of the best jams and home-made cakes you'll ever taste. Daisies add a poetic touch to a country still life of a tap and fence.*

Piketberg and surrounds

Piketberg sits in a sea of winter green wheat and summer gold harvest at the foot of the Piket Berg. There are smudgy blue mountains in the distance, creaking windmills and dusty farm roads leading to the town. It has all the elements of a small South African farming *dorpie* – big wide main road, a sprinkling of shops, a chicken takeaway and a *bakkie* dealership. Piketberg comes alive on a Saturday when seasonal farm workers stream in to spend their hard-earned cash. It's peaceful, not a helluva lot happens, and that's exactly why people love it.

Life in the area wasn't always so peaceful and the town's name gives a hint of its turbulent past. Piketberg started out with a more French spelling from the word *piquet*, which refers to a small group of soldiers commissioned to guard a lookout post. Early farmers were vulnerable to attack by the indigenous tribes and in 1792 a lookout was established on the farm Honingberg in an attempt to quell the looting that took place.

Piketberg attracted not only farmers, but many Jewish settlers who had come from Lithuania. It's hard to know what drew them here rather than elsewhere, but there was soon a thriving community and today the former synagogue serves as the local tourism information bureau. Although many of the immigrants were penniless when they arrived from Eastern Europe, there are more than a few stories of men who started out as itinerant *smouse* travelling dusty back roads from farm to farm who went on to become enormously successful entrepreneurs. To honour their past, descendants of Piketberg's original Jewish community came back in 2004 to participate in a symbolic olive tree planting ceremony.

This spread *The blue-tinged Piketberg mountains tower over a landscape that changes with the seasons. In winter you'll drive through a sea of green wheat, while in summer the fields are swathed in golden grain ready for harvest. In spring, when the daisies and other wild flowers take turns to show off their colours, you'll be hard-pressed to find prettier country scenes.*

You can't visit Piketberg without going to the pretty Piket-Bo-Berg via the impressive Versfeld Pass. As you wind your way up the looping pass, you'll quickly develop an appreciation for the amount of labour that went into building this road. The original pass was built in the late 1880s using only picks, shovels and an enormous amount of sweat. No explosives shortcuts were taken and the large loops had to be carefully designed to accommodate the ox wagons that trundled up and down with valuable supplies. A new pass that also bends back on itself was built by J.P.E. Versveld in the 1950s – even though the noise from the whips and sound of oxen straining against their traces has long since gone.

By all accounts, Versveld was something of a Renaissance man. He was handsome, musical, fond of poetry, had a good singing voice, was a pioneering farmer and an intrepid civil engineer whose road helped open up an area that had been written off as inaccessible and dangerous.

Never content to follow what other farmers were doing, Versveld branched into ostrich farming and made a small fortune. He worked in partnership with his brother-in-law, Peter van Breda, who lived at Geelbek, the historic homestead in the West Coast National Park *(see pg 68)*. He was so successful that he even bought a town house in Wynberg to which his family could escape and be a part of the Cape social scene.

The collapse of the feather trade in 1885, however, meant a move back to the farm on the mountain and it was then that Versveld decided to tackle the pass. Patrick Carter from Excelsior farm, just across the way from the old Versveld farm, recounts that the inspiration for the design of the pass came when Versveld dropped his fob chain. As it fell, it looped back on itself, and Versveld realised how he could tackle the steep gradient. It took him and 20 labourers just three months to hack a safe route up the mountain. Of course, once this was done, transport improved enormously and Piketberg no longer seemed so remote and full of foreboding.

not a helluva lot happens

Piket-bo-berg Tea Garden

Henny Visser hates sitting around doing nothing, which is why she convinced her son and husband to build her a small tea garden on their farm among the hills and valleys of the Piketberg. Her son farms lavender, tomatoes and gorgeous fuchsias that he sells to nurseries in and around Cape Town, and Henny keeps herself busy serving delicious home-made cakes to hungry passers-by at the aptly-named Piket-bo-berg Tea Garden.

Her ginger beer, perfect for a sweltering summer's day, is legendary, as is her sweet potato cake *(see right)*.

Home-made ginger beer (20 litres)

2,5kg sugar
kettle full of boiling water
100g fresh yeast (ask your bakery)
1 teaspoon sugar
50ml Jamaica ginger

Put a whole packet (2,5kg) sugar and a kettle full of boiling water into a 20 litre bucket. Stir well until the sugar is dissolved. In a cup, place the yeast and 1 teaspoon of sugar with a little lukewarm water and stir until well combined. Leave to stand until foam has formed. Add Jamaica ginger to bucket. Put in the yeast mixture and start adding cold water until the bucket is full, stirring now and then. Once all ingredients are mixed together, it is ready to decant into 2-litre bottles. Seal tightly and leave for a minimum of 8 hours. The longer it stands, the more fermentation takes place and the bubblier it becomes.

Previous spread *Each year the Piketberg Agricultural Show pulls in the crowds who are happiest in khaki farmer gear and vellies. One of the highlights is the potjiekos challenge during which competitors get to down lots of brandy and Coke and comparing their favourite recipes. Blushing Bride proteas are gathered in a delicate posy.*

This spread *Icons of early spring: snow-capped mountains, green fields and a carpet of daisies.*

Sweet potato cake

550ml unsifted cake flour
1 tablespoon baking powder
1 teaspoon cinnamon
1 teaspoon ground nutmeg
1ml salt
2 cups sugar
1½ cups sunflower oil
60ml boiling water
4 eggs, separated
1½ cups peeled, coarsely grated sweet potatoes
1 cup chopped walnuts
1 teaspoon vanilla essence

Filling and icing

2 cups sifted icing sugar
60ml butter or margarine, at room temperature
1 tub smooth cottage cheese
½ cup chopped walnuts
a little cinnamon

Preheat oven to 180°C. Grease three 23cm diameter layer cake tins and dust them with cake flour, or spray them with non-stick cooking spray.

Sift together the flour, baking powder, cinnamon, nutmeg and salt. Beat the sugar and sunflower oil together well. Add the boiling water and continue beating until the water has been completely incorporated. Add the egg yolks and flour mixture and stir to combine. Add the sweet potatoes, walnuts and vanilla essence and mix. Beat the egg whites until stiff and fold them lightly into the sweet potato mixture with a metal spoon. Spoon the batter into the cake tins and level them off. Bake for ±40 minutes. Allow the cake layers to cool slightly in the tins. Then turn them out carefully onto wire racks to cool completely.

Combine the icing sugar and butter, or margarine, well – the mixture will resemble fine crumbs. Add half the cottage cheese and stir until just combined. Spread the remaining cottage cheese on top of each cake layer. Spread the cottage cheese icing on top of the cottage cheese and sandwich the layers together. Sprinkle the walnuts on top, around the edge, and sift a little cinnamon in the centre. Cool the cake briefly in the refrigerator before serving. Store in the refrigerator.

Master OF
THE
MOUNTAIN
Take deep breath and
thrust
board
Pure
A cold SNOW

Tamarak Protea Farm

Tamarak Farm is just one of the protea farms on the West Coast. Situated at the end of Langeberg Road, it's perched on the edge of the Piketberg. The view over Koringberg and on to Kasteelberg is fantastic. On a clear day you can see Simonsberg in the distance and, if you're lucky, Table Mountain far away.

Paul and Anniza de Villiers bought the farm 10 years ago and, although they both still work at their other 'townie' careers as consultants in different sectors, started farming proteas about four years ago. Chat to any farmer and they'll echo the same sentiments: protea farming ain't as easy as it looks.

Sure, proteas are indigenous and look pretty hardy but they're also sensitive souls that might do fantastically well on one slope but fail to thrive on another just a few kilometres away. They're also prone to a fungus called *Phytophthora* that lives in the soil and attacks the plants' roots.

'One day your bushes are flourishing and the next, they're dead,' comments Paul. 'The fungus is present in the soil water where proteas grow wild, but when you start cultivating them, there are a lot of plants concentrated in one area and this makes them susceptible to disease. Treatment is expensive and doesn't last long. Prevention is better than cure and ensuring that your soil is well drained is one of the steps you can take to minimise damage caused by the disease. It is also important to select proteas that are suitable to your area.'

There are more than 360 proteas that are endemic to South Africa. Although the West Coast is crammed with protea species, there are only about 20 that are endemic to the region. The majority is grown to be sold as export cut flowers to Europe – a valuable multi-million rand industry.

But it's not all plain sailing. One of the biggest challenges protea farmers face is dealing with the Cape sugarbirds, which hone in on the blooms. 'They are incredibly strong and will pick open a bloom to get to the sweet nectar within,' explains Anniza.

'They have long brush-tipped tongues and really sharp claws that allow them to hang onto a stem while they get to work. For a bird that small, they can do an enormous amount of damage. It's labour intensive, but we cover our blooms with paper pie bags,' she elaborates. 'You can also use stockings but we just buy these offcuts from the factory and they're fairly easy to put on.'

The names of the proteas are as gorgeous as the blooms. There's the *Protea magnifica* with its dark inner eye and white-tipped petals; the appropriately delicate pink Lady Di; the fiery red Venus and, of course, the commanding pink King Protea (*Protea cynaroides*) with its open face and downy white centre.

Previous spread *Young Jared Whitfield from Piketberg-Bo-Berg is master of the mountain and has grown up surrounded by buchu and proteas.*

Spring has just touched the mountain and the first blossoms can be seen on these fruit trees, which will soon explode into a white frothiness.

This spread *People in Europe pay a small fortune for our exported flowers. Country bunches of* fynbos *put store-bought flowers to shame at the Piketberg Agricultural Show.*

look pretty hardy but they're also sensitive souls

Renosterbos – rough as a rhino's hide

Although most of the fertile soils of the Swartland and Sandveld are cultivated for farming, look out for the few remaining patches of *renosterveld,* which you'll usually find in the valleys that tractors and harvesters can't get to – or in areas given over to conservation.

Renosterveld is dominated by members of the Daisy family (Asteraceae) and is also often referred to as *renosterbos* after one of the dominant species – *Elytropappus rhinocerotis*. There's some debate about the name's origin, however; some people believe it came from the black rhino that used to graze on it, while others think it is from the grey shrub's resemblance to the tough rhino hide. *Renosterveld* vegetation is incredibly diverse and plentiful and contains 1 036 species of daisy, 760 species of pea, 661 species of iris, 418 species of snapdragon, 227 species of orchid and 660 species of *vygie*. Grasses are also abundant.

Renosterbos and some other *renosterveld* species have tiny leaves coated with a waxy substance that helps reduce water loss but it burns well, even when green, and has often been used for fuel. *Renosterbos* is also used medicinally to alleviate the flu and typhoid.

That *renosterveld* typically grows on fertile soil has largely been its downfall as most of these areas have been ploughed for wheat and stock farming. The last study undertaken to assess the status of this vegetation type was completed in 2003 and at that stage only 5% remained.

Green gold

Buchu has a reputation as a miracle cure-all. You got it, buchu can fix it. It is so valuable it's known as 'green gold'. Used by indigenous people and early settlers, it has been around for ages, which only adds to its mystique and reputation. Chat to any Sandvelder and they'll tell you stories of how when their *Oupa* Loos got kicked by a horse and was on his deathbed, they administered a good dose of buchu brandy and he was up and about in a matter of hours. Or of *Ouma* Griekie who treated every stomach ailment with buchu tea and lived to be a *fris* 98 years.

Seriously, though, buchu is reputed to be particularly good for urinary tract infections and kidney disorders. Others say it's excellent for treating muscular pain because it reduces inflammation, while others swear that it can rid you of rheumatism, prostate problems, kidney stones and high blood pressure. Diabetes, HIV/AIDS, colds and flu are also on the list.

So, what's the fuss? If buchu has been around forever, what's to stop it growing for decades to come? Plenty, it seems. What used to be a great local product used in home remedies has attracted international interest, and this seems to be where the problem lies. Although there are 132 species of buchu, there are only two that are primarily used commercially: *Agathosma betulina* and *Agathosma crenulata*. It's buchu's fixative property that is currently making everybody sit up and take notice. Although most people find this surprising to believe because of the plant's pungent smell, buchu is used in the soft drink industry as a flavourant. It's also used in perfume

'You got it, buchu can fix it'

manufacturing to ensure the volatile compounds are more stable, allowing fragrances to keep their scent longer.

The South African buchu market brings in millions of rands each year. However, there's talk of certain easy-to-reach populations of plants being 'poached out' of the nature reserves and mountain areas. Marta de Ponte Machado, a researcher at the University of Cape Town, wrote a thesis on buchu and is quick to allay these fears. 'I think it's unlikely that buchu is being driven to the brink of extinction,' she explains, 'but the increased demand has certainly changed the way people think about the plant and altered the way it is being harvested.'

There's no doubt that there's increased pressure on buchu that is easily accessible and the impact of harvesting was just one of the aspects that Marta investigated. 'Buchu has a complicated storage root system and if the leaves are cut too often, this root loses out on valuable energy and dies because the plant just never has enough time to recover.'

The simple response would be to harvest every other year, but this is where social issues come in to play and complicate the picture. With the growing demand for buchu, it's not unheard of for neighbours to poach from one another, or for harvesters to come from the city and move through a patch of buchu in the middle of the night. Farmers are quick to blame Rastafarians who use the plant extensively, but for many people, the fact that the plants are wild denotes a sense of common ownership and entitlement. Land claims have also had an impact as people have moved back into areas, and begun harvesting buchu.

To meet the growing demand, extensive buchu plantations are being established, but this has also generated mixed feelings. Often huge tracts of pristine *fynbos* are cleared for the buchu. Sure, it's an indigenous crop, but there's the argument that any form of monoculture doesn't do the ecology any good. There are some examples of people growing buchu under the *fynbos*, just clearing enough to be able to grow the seedlings but Marta is unaware of the yield or the success rate of these experiments.

'There's a great deal of research being done into buchu cultivation. It's important to establish if cultivated buchu has the same properties as buchu that grows in the wild. Fortunately, I think there will always be pockets of buchu that won't be tampered with because they are in such remote places, but there's still no room for complacency.'

Look out for buchu products such as teas, loose leaves, soaps and body creams at West Coast farm stalls. Winkelshoek Curio Shop and Farm Stall, on the N7 near the turn off to Piketberg, sells buchu teabags that make for a pungent-smelling and robust drink that's more health-giving than tasty.

This spread *Piketberg-Bo-Berg farmer Rob Whitfield knows this unprepossessing plant has plenty to offer, which is why it's so sought-after and now under threat of over-harvesting.*

Hopefield and surrounds

Like so many small South African farming towns, Hopefield has hidden charms. You could drive past it without giving it a second glance but it's certainly worth attending a service in the Dutch Reformed Church, which dominates the town. The town's residents are justifiably proud of the organ that takes pride of place in the church. One of only 12 of its kind that were bought to South Africa between 1910 and 1912, it produces a rich, warm sound that will certainly make you believe in angels. Also well worth a visit is the *fynbos* flower display that the town hosts in the last weekend of August each year when the four different types of *fynbos* endemic to the area are displayed in the sports' hall. And, if you feel like treating yourself, be sure to spend a night at Kersefontein, one of the historic farms in the area, which now also offers luxury accommodation.

Kersefontein

Julian Melck's business card is a tad unusual. 'Farmer, Pig-killer, Aviator, Advocate of the High Court of SA,' it reads. In that order. But then again, Julian is an unusual man with a rich legacy. He's the eighth generation Melck to farm Kersefontein, a magnificent 6 000ha estate on the banks of the Berg River. The farm was originally bought in 1770 by Martin Melck, a settler who more than made good in his new country. The first deed described the farm as '*zeker Veepost*' or 'certain cattle post' and that's exactly what Martin Melck intended to use it for – additional grazing for his growing herds of cattle and flocks of sheep.

Martin Melck was born in Memel in Prussia, but as a young man joined the Dutch East India Company to escape the growing economic hardships in Europe. Despatched to the Cape in 1746, he began building his fortune. He was an astute businessman who, after just three decades in the Colony, was one of its most prominent citizens. In 1776, Melck and his wife's estate was listed as: 10 farms, 203 slaves, 170 horses, 1 321 cattle, 4 167 sheep and 106 pigs.

Melck was wealthy, but also highly principled and refused to give up his Lutheran faith to appease the Dutch who had declared that the only permitted place of worship in the Colony was in the Dutch Reformed Church.

In 1774, Melck built a barn in Strand Street. It was supposedly a store for his goods but was, in fact, used as a place of worship. He built a parsonage next to the barn, and later a town house in the same complex. The house was designed by well-known architect of the time, Anton Anreith, and had the unusual addition of a *dakkamer*, a room built in the roof, which allowed the wealthy merchant to see when ships sailed into the bay. The three buildings were declared National Monuments in the late 1940s and today Martin Melck House is home to the spectacular Gold of Africa Museum. In 1779 the government in

Amsterdam finally granted Lutherans permission to worship freely, and an elaborate pulpit was installed in 'the barn'.

The original Martin Melck was a hard act to follow and not all the subsequent custodians of Kersefontein were as business-minded. At one point around 1810, high living got the better of one couple. The debts they accumulated were so great that two other historic farms owned by the family, Elsenberg (now the agricultural college in Stellenbosch) and St Helenasfontein, had to be sold off. Today Kersefontein, named after the wild cherries or *kerse* that grow on the farm, has a calm and settled air about it. The buildings are solid and whitewashed, rounded at the corners with strong, comforting contours.

Julian Melck started farming in the mid-80s. While he's still planting and reaping grain, and raising cattle and sheep like most of his forefathers, he has transformed the outbuildings into an elegant B&B where the rich and famous retreat for peace and quiet and fine dining. The man is a brilliant host: a great raconteur, more than a little eccentric and enormously smart. If you're lucky, he'll shoot a wild boar for dinner or, depending on the season, treat you to the Red Gold of the West Coast – delicate crayfish served at room temperature with a delicious dipping sauce. You're luckier still if he plays the piano after dinner, but you'll have hit the jackpot if he makes the trip with you to the Hopefield church to play the organ.

'The organ is a big instrument,' says Julian in passing on his way out to the fields. 'There's passion, complexity and richness in its sound. I'm a bit of an exhibitionist so it suits my personality perfectly.'

The history that Julian has inherited pervades every aspect of Kersefontein. Dotted throughout the house are old photos of Julian's father, Martin, showing one of his merino sheep; there's a beautiful sepia print of a good-looking woman dressed in racing silks on a shiny mount – Julian's mother who was an excellent rider and former jockey; and an enormous hippopotamus skull from the last animal in the area which was shot by Julian's great-grandfather in front of the house in February 1869. The gun is mounted just feet away. There are oil paintings of the house dating back centuries, and paintings of the people who have worked there.

Trained as an advocate, Julian wasn't always going to farm, but the love of the land and the pull of the farm soon proved too strong. 'There's something very creative about farming,' he reflects. 'It's the simple act of growing something, but then there's also something beautiful about the patterns you make on the earth and the aesthetics of how things look.'

This spread *Kersefontein's Julian Melck keeps an eye on winter grain planting, but can also sometimes be found at the organ at Hopefield church. The old graveyard on the farm has a commanding view over the fields and homestead.*

Kersefontein leg of wild boar

1 leg (or saddle) of wild boar
15ml butter or lard
15ml oil
2 onions, quartered
2 cans apple cider (Hunters or Savanna)
salt and pepper to taste
a few bay leaves
a few cloves
a few peppercorns

Using an *oondkastrol* (roaster with lid), seal meat in butter or lard and oil, and sauté onions. Add cider, seasoning, bay leaves, cloves and peppercorns. Cover and cook in 180–200°C oven for about 3 hours, basting occasionally. Remove lid for last half hour to brown meat. Serve with stewed apples and seasonal vegetables. Serves 8 to 12 persons, depending on size and how hungry everyone is.

Previous spread *The textured doors and window shutters at Kersefontein speak of years of use. Early morning dew hangs on an old gate hook at Kersefontein.*

This spread *Young Dawid Lingerveld helps his father, Hendrik, in the Kersefontein dairy when he's home for the school holidays and over weekends. He's also in charge of feeding the orphaned lambs, which Hendrik fetches off the veld on horseback. It's no surprise that the wobbly lambs follow David around at every opportunity, along with the farm cats that make the dairy their home.*

Pigs on the run

The feral pigs Julian hunts aren't just any regular porkers. They're domestic pigs that escaped years ago from the Kersefontein pigsties and have gone on to breed and live in the *veld* and tall reeds that hug the banks of the Berg River. They have even made it into *The Mammals of the Southern African Subregion* (New Edition) by J.D. Skinner and R.H.N. Smithers, and are known formally as Kersefontein feral pig.

You can join Julian on the boar hunt if you have nerves of steel and a strong constitution, or you can stay up at the house and wait for the bloody act to be over and done with. He goes into graphic detail: 'Boar hunting is done on foot. The best time to shoot pigs is at dusk, or the early morning, as they are nocturnal, and suspicious animals. They don't have a great sense of hearing or seeing, but you dare not be upwind of one, because their sense of smell is fantastic (the reason why pigs are used to look for truffles in France).

'We go for the big boars, and try and avoid shooting the sows, especially if they are carrying, or caring for, young. Sometimes a group of us will chase up the young, up to, say, bull-terrier size, dive on them and catch them. They are then put in a wheat-bag, and brought home to the sty. It's a *lekker boeresport*! They breed well and have a high libido, the envy of many a human. They graze on anything, especially roots, are omnivores, like humans, and love carrion. They will pick a dead sheep clean. They cause a huge amount of damage in cereal crops, rolling the wheat flat so that they can eat the ripe ears from the ground. No combine harvester can pick up wheat where pigs have been.

'I use both a light- and a heavy-calibre rifle to shoot pigs, preferably with sharp-point, military-style rounds, so that there is little damage to the meat. This requires a fair amount of accuracy. Pigs are tough and don't die easily, so a wounded pig is usually administered the *coup de grâce* with a handgun. I have been charged a number of times and have, on occasion, had to flee an angry pig. They are bad-tempered, like their cousins, the hippo. We – myself, friends, guests and staff – eat everything, from the brains to the trotters. The best cut is a leg, or better still, a saddle of wild boar. Just ask Obelix, Asterix's friend.'

And, once you've returned to Kersefontein, indulged in a stiff drink and a long hot bath, you can expect to enjoy the famous roast boar recipe that evening.

pret in die

Two birds flying high,
A Chinese vessel, sailing by.
A bridge with three men, sometimes four,
A willow tree, hanging o'er.
A Chinese temple, there it stands,
Built upon the river sands.
An apple tree, with apples on,
A crooked fence to end my song.

Willow pattern pieces

Kick around in the dirt behind one of the historic West Coast homes and you may find some unusual treasure buried in the sandy soil – shards of cobalt blue and white Willow pattern pottery dating back to the late 1700s. It's hardly surprising that you'll find these fragments in far-flung places throughout the Western Cape, from the Constantia green belt to a plot in Kalk Bay to behind the barn at Kersefontein. When the Dutch and British settled in the Cape Colony they brought with them one of the most fashionable china designs of the time – the Willow pattern.

There are a number of poems written about the Willow pattern but it's not entirely clear if the legend developed in England or China. It tells the story of two forbidden lovers who have to escape the wrath of the woman's father, a rich old Mandarin, who has promised his daughter to a wealthy suitor. Contrary to his wishes, she's fallen in love with one of his employees. The pattern depicts a garden with the two young lovers being chased over the bridge by the old man. In some designs they're chased by the father and the suitor, so the number of people on the bridge varies. They make it to a teahouse, but disaster follows when the Mandarin sets the place on fire and the two lovers burn to death. Their spirits escape, however, and are transformed into two doves, which hover out of reach.

The pretty shards are a reminder of days gone by when sailing ships plied the treacherous route from Europe, to Cape Town and then on to the East.

Veld finds

Take a walk across the *sandveld* and you'll find plenty of evidence of porcupines. Scuffle marks in the ground show where they've found edible bulbs and roots and, if that's not proof enough, they have around 3 000 stripy quills, which they regularly leave as calling cards. Porcupines grow to around 60cm long and weigh in at anything between 18 and 30kg. There are stories from Kersefontein of porcupines bustling down the passage, quills rustling as they go, in search of dog food. And at least one city visitor has been woken to find a prickly guest at the end of the bed!

Even before Hildagonda Duckitt's *Hilda's Where is it?* *(see pg 47)* caused a stir among Cape housewives, Great-aunt Allie's *Cape Cookery: Simple yet Distinctive* – the first cookery book published in South Africa – was released by Darter's in 1890 in Cape Town. *Cape Cookery* ran to six editions between 1890 and 1911, and was out of print for more than 60 years when A.G. Hewitt resurrected his great-aunt's recipes and published a book of these in 1973.

Aunt Allie had plenty to say about porcupines, which she believed wreaked havoc among gardens throughout the Cape: 'Porcupines harass farmers throughout the Republic and neighbouring states, the only areas where they are not found being the desert and semi-desert regions of the northern Cape and South West Africa. This animal is still regarded as a pest and to be kept down. What happens to the carcasses when they are shot? Ask the farm-labourers; they will tell you. The fact is that porcupine is not impossible to come by once in a while.

'Most of us can boast a friend or a friend of a friend who farms where this animal is found. It is more than worthwhile to go to the trouble of acquiring one. Roast porcupine, as a gastronomic experience, is unique *(see below)*. If one says that the flavour is like a combination of suckling pig and duck with just a hint of venison about it, the story is not half told. It would be far less costly and more fitting to serve roast porcupine at State banquets to honour special visitors to our country than to fly out caviare from one of the lands bordering on the Black Sea.'

Aunt Allie's porcupine preparation

When the quills have been taken out the porcupine it must be scalded and scraped to remove the hair.

When well cleaned, take the skin of the animal, which is considered the prime part, wash it, and lay it in salt and water with pepper, until the next day.

Put it on to boil in fresh water and cook it gently until quite soft. Cut it into neat pieces and broil them over a charcoal fire. Serve with butter and sliced lemon.

The flesh may be stewed or roasted, whole or in parts, and is very delicate in flavour. The seasoning should be that used for suckling pig.

This spread *Finding shards of blue and white willow pattern pottery is always exciting and the pieces surface in the most surprising places, from Constantia through to Hopefield. Some of the pottery dates back to the early days of the Colony when this style of china was all the rage.*

Porterville and surrounds

The little town of Porterville isn't going to stop you dead with excitement. It's a typical West Coast town with a bank, a couple of bottle stores, grain offices and a few cafés lining the main road. Yawn too long and you might miss it. But this doesn't mean it's without charm – and that's what makes towns off the beaten track so appealing. It was established in 1863 when one of the original 1820 Settlers, Frederick John Owen, subdivided his farm into *erven*. The town was named after the popular Attorney General of the Cape, William Porter. The area was incredibly fertile and the many rivers that coursed down the Olifantsriver Mountains meant the local farms had all the water they needed to farm successfully. In the early days, a herd of around 400 elephant roamed the plains and a local Porterviller says white 'tigers' sought shelter in the craggy mountains. A local conservationist believes it's highly unlikely that the animals were genuinely tigers as they aren't indigenous to Africa. A more plausible explanation is that these were lighter-coloured leopards.

Today some of the original farms still exist, but since the late 1940s lack of water has been a major problem for farmers in the area. The weather patterns have changed, the winters are drier than they used to be and the summers appear longer and hotter. A canal runs from the Voëlvlei dam to service nearby farms, but one farmer complained that any attempts to organise farmers around a shared water scheme was like pushing frogs in a wheelbarrow: 'Just when you get going, one jumps out and you've got to start all over again.'

Porterville's real treasures lie outside the town. The climb up Dasklip Pass is breathtaking. Until it was tarred a few years ago, it was a lot more treacherous. But, if you can contain your nerves till you reach the top, it's worth it. On a clear day you look out across the *vlaktes* of wheat fields and canola to the mountains of the Riebeek Valley and beyond to Simonsberg near Stellenbosch. On misty days, when the vistas come and go like the twirling and ever-changing images in a kaleidoscope, then you might catch a glimpse of a white farmhouse with a red roof, a splash of yellow and a swathe of green before the fog closes in, and then all you see is a quiet whiteness and the back of your hand.

Up and over the pass is the Groot Winterhoek Nature Reserve, a hikers' paradise. There's also the somewhat eccentric Beaverlac holiday resort on Grootfontein Farm. The area has been declared a South African Natural Heritage Site and the endless rock pools and *fynbos* are astonishing. Staying there, though, is a bit like taking a step back into a trippy, hippy sort of world where all the campers seem to wear tie-dyed T-shirts in summer and woolly beanies in winter.

This spread *During winter, after the rains have lashed the Cape, this farm dam near Porterville swells and the landscape takes on a scrubbed look. Keep an eye out for home-made* melktert *and the more lethal* witblits *when visiting local farmers.*

KOEKE-
MAKRANKA
IN WITBLITS
NOT FOR
SALE

Disa uniflora – lady in red

If you're hiking in the mountains in the Porterville area, keep an eye open for the beautiful *Disa uniflora*, which flourishes on these boggy mountains and *vleis*. Disas are part of the orchid family, and according to Dr Hubert Kurzweil, orchid expert from the South African National Biodiversity Institute (SANBI), it is an almost entirely African genus. One species ranges into Yemen, three are endemic to Madagascar and one is found only in Réunion.

The World Checklist of Monocotyledons, published by the Royal Botanic Gardens, Kew, is a directory of plants and their distribution. The checklist, which is continually updated, records 174 disa species, including three natural hybrids that occur only sporadically. Interestingly, at the beginning of 2004 a pretty white and pink new species was found in the Hex River Mountains. This has been sent to a disa expert for verification and, once this has been confirmed, then perhaps there'll be 175 species in total.

The possible origin of the name is as elusive as these pretty plants, which thrive in the coolness of cascades and waterfalls. The first European botanist to describe the disa genus was Petrus Jonas Bergius who in 1767 examined a specimen and was intrigued by the fine net-like veins on the red sepals. It is believed that the name comes from a Swedish myth in which a beautiful woman, Disa, came to the king dressed in a lovely fishnet gown.

The most common species, though, is *D. uniflora*, which is also known as the Pride of Table Mountain, Flower of the Gods or, more modestly, Red Disa. Most people are not aware that this is the flower emblem emblazoned on Western Province rugby jerseys.

Much as Disa enthralled the ancient king, today *D. uniflora* attracts the large Mountain Pride Butterfly (*Meneris tulbaghia*), which is drawn to the flower's startling red display. The disa species is one of only a handful of plant species pollinated by this butterfly, which is a fool for anything red – including backpacks, red hiking socks or scarlet T-shirts. According to experts, red is a colour many other insects don't register.

You might also find some yellow disas on your rambles. According to Dr Kurzweil, 'The yellow form of the Red Disa is very rare in nature, and does not reproduce as its colour does not attract the Mountain Pride Butterfly, and consequently it is not pollinated. It is simply a sporadic mutation where the red pigment is not present.'

As tempted as you may be, remember that disas are stringently protected and it is illegal to pick or damage them.

Dasklip – flying high

There's a moment when you step off the launch ramp and into thin air when it must feel like death or dying – or at least close. The sense of sheer adrenalin, hearing your heart pounding in your ears and then the tug of your harness as the elements take over and you're airborne. Flying. Soaring. On the wing.

Excitement and adventure made real: Porterville is a fabulous hang- and paragliding region. It's got so much going for it. Brilliant thermals that start coming through in September and just keep getting better throughout summer, and a really long ridge of mountains, which means great flying right up towards Citrusdal, Clanwilliam and beyond.

There's all the airspace any pilot could hope for. Since Porterville is far away from major cities, there's little chance of getting in the way of incoming aeroplanes, or landing on a busy highway. Bradley Meyer has been flying for four years and is one of the partners at Porterville Flyer's Lodge, an old Victorian farmhouse on the edge of the town. Pilots from all over the world flock to this mecca of free flying, and during peak season the Lodge starts to look like the United Nations on a busy day.

'Dasklip is probably the only site in South Africa where you fly such distances for so much of the year,' explains Bradley with enthusiasm. 'During competitions we routinely fly between 80 and 120km for a task. The views from 3 000m are amazing. But there's not always time to relax; and flying has claimed more than its fair share of casualties. With these very advanced gliders there's often very little room for error. Interestingly, the pilots who have died in the last few years have all been very experienced, but appear to have misjudged the wind and thermal conditions in the area over which they flew.

'However, there are moments of sheer bliss when you are hanging suspended above an elliptical world made up of wheat fields and mountains. Flying above the farms, you hear all the animal sounds, the tractors and machinery and the workers chatting. You can even smell the farm odours in the rising thermals. When you're very high, all you can hear is the whistling of the wind in your lines. For long moments it's very peaceful, but when you are once again approaching the ground you've got to start thinking about where to land. You don't want to land in a tree or crash into telephone wires!'

This spread *The spectacular Dasklip Pass just outside Porterville is a hang- and paragliders' paradise, and has many different moods, depending on the time of year and wind conditions.*

Jaco van Deventer – man with a mission

CapeNature's Jaco van Deventer is a nice guy, but some of the people he gets to deal with are not. Jaco is based at the somnambulant Porterville but, as one of the main conservation figures in the area, he rarely gets to doze off. Just one aspect of his very busy job involves helping CapeNature Conservation's Environmental Crime Investigation Unit (ECIS).

Environmental crime, which internationally ranks second after drug trafficking, has hit South Africa and the Western Cape particularly hard. Our country is rich in natural resources and inevitably (and unfortunately) there are always people who want those things that are rare and endangered. The colophon beetle is a prize example, and in 2003 Jaco and his colleagues bust a large-scale beetle-smuggling ring.

'People always think we're a bit crazy when we get worked up about colophon beetles,' the good-looking ranger laughs, 'but they are highly endangered and are only found on the mountain peaks in this region and they are so specialised that you might find one species living in an area the size of your office or a room in your house.'

The beetle is so rare that in 1999 the South African Government had it listed as an endangered species. 'Colophon beetles have been around for millennia,' Jaco continues. 'They're the dinosaurs of the insect world and have survived two Ice Ages. With global warming, the beetle retreated to mountain peaks and has adapted to survive in small pockets. According to information some species populations are extremely small.'

Which goes some way to explain why Jaco and his colleagues were so upset when they caught four 'tourists' with over 200 dead colophon beetles. The arrest would make for a good movie script. 'We received a tip off and acted on that,' he explains. 'Not much is known about these beetles and the poachers know far more than most experts and this gives them an edge. The beetles live underground for most of the year and only come out for a few weeks in summer to mate. When the eggs hatch, the larvae remain in the soil for several years and they're really difficult to find.'

But not difficult enough to deter international smugglers who come equipped with highly specialised insect-collecting equipment.

'Together with the police we set up a roadblock and caught the guys coming off the mountain. You could see that they were pretty nervous when we caught them, but it's obvious this is what they do to make a really good living. The one guy had a roll of euros in his side pocket so they were clearly big players. We found documents linking them to other countries in Africa and to a contact in Ladismith. They were very slick operators. They kill the beetles and then just post them out of the country to dealers around the world.'

For collectors, this beetle is the cherry on the top. 'The colophon are the most expensive you can buy. The guys were caught with a total of 212 colophon beetles and 842 specimens of other insects, and seven scorpions. The beetles were dead, but the scorpions were alive.'

Paul Gildenhuys, the Environmental Crime Investigation Unit manager, explains that they have successfully prosecuted nearly 250 cases since the unit was formed at the end of 2001. Some of the other cases that have made newspaper headlines included the theft of more than 500 *Hawthornia* dwarf aloes and angulate tortoises. 'Tragically,' Paul discloses, '90% of all reptiles smuggled overseas die within the first year.'

The unit splits its tasks into two areas of fauna and flora. The biggest problems locally are poaching of game, and the illegal keeping of primates and the country's national bird, the blue crane.

This spread *Beaverlac holiday resort near Porterville is a good place to disappear to when you need to leave the city behind and recharge your batteries. The chalets are rudimentary, but if you like camping, you'll be able to find a lovely spot under the trees. In spring, the* fynbos *is astonishing, but in summer you won't want to leave the river and the enormous rock pools that make this place so special.*

the perfume is so
like peach or

The traditional bredie

Waterblommetjies are as much a part of the West Coast landscape as *bokkoms,* spring flowers and stunning sunsets. You'll see the pretty white flowers sprinkled across dams and *vleis* when the cold winter rains have lashed the Cape and filled up any dips and hollows in the land. In the summer, when the *veld* is blisteringly dry, it is hard to imagine how they arrive unannounced – but most welcome – every year.

The much-loved South African performer Anton Goosen sang:

'Waterblommetjies in die Boland
Waterblommetjies in die Kaap
Maak die bredie net soos in die wynland
En sê jy's baie lief vir my
Voor jy gaan slaap'

These aquatic plants are not difficult to grow and they seed themselves, which makes them a pretty low-maintenance crop. Collecting them on an icy winter's morning when there's snow on the mountains just outside Porterville is an entirely different story, however. The water is bone-achingly cold and standing waist high in pond water is numbing work. But Klaas 'Solly' Miller, from the farm Môrester, has been harvesting *blommetjies* for years and works his way methodically through the dam.

'*Waterblommetjies* always come out at the same time as the arum lily,' says Isobel van Niekerk, the farm's matriarch. Isobel is one of those incredible women that seem to thrive in country towns. She's warm, wise, cooks like a dream, does woodwork in her spare time and can sew a fine thread. And she helps her son, Chris, farm watermelons, *spanspek* and goats and has as much energy as 10 women half her age. When the winter rains lash the Cape and the *waterblommetjie* season begins, Isobel has a small business supplying supermarkets with this Cape delicacy. Though now sought-after, '*waterblommetjies* are not fancy food,' Isobel acknowledges. 'Coloured families grew up looking for food from the *veld* and we learnt from them. Smell the flowers,' she encourages. 'The perfume is so delicate – much like peach or plum blossoms. On warm winter days the scent rises off the dams and is so wonderful. And if you open a bag of freshly picked *waterblommetjies,* you'll also catch a passing whiff. When the first *waterblommetjies* of the season appear, I always pick a few to put in a vase on the dining room table. It reminds me of the coming spring.'

According to experts, *Aponogeton distachyos* is pretty hardy and was first cultivated in Europe in the 17th century, although it's hard to imagine something so typically South African growing anywhere other than home soil, or rather home water. The plant is perfectly adapted to ponds and *vleis* that dry up in summer and the best time to pick them is from July through to September. The dormant tubers come to life again when the first winter rains fill up the ponds.

'But the landscape is changing so much,' Isobel comments. 'The *vleis* that I remember as a child have long since dried up and there never seems to be enough rain to fill the dams. The porcupines also move through the dried *vleis* during summer and dig up the bulbs. So do people, because you can eat the bulbs like potatoes.'

The aroma from Isobel's kitchen is comforting. There are two freshly made *melkterte* on the table, a collection of muffins and *waterblommetjiebredie* on the stove *(see opposite)*.

'They say that the way to a man's heart is through his stomach,' smiles

delicate – much plum blossoms

this wife and mother sagely. 'The thing about *waterblommetjiebredie* is that you can't rush it. You can't decide that you want to make a *bredie* at 10:30 and expect it to be ready by 12:30. Ideally you should cook it on an old Dover stove rather than an electric one. You should also cook when you are calm and relaxed,' she continues. 'That way your attitude gets transferred to the food you're preparing. I don't envy young families today. Everybody is so rushed and there's no time to take things slowly. *Rustigheid* is very important and an integral part of being a woman.'

Chris van Niekerk is critically aware of old-fashioned values and, together with his mother, is trying to farm in harmony with nature. His brother farms organically next door and they're going to be replanting *kalkoentjies*, an indigenous flower, on a hillock on the farm that's known as Kalkoenkop.

Isobel also has some highly prized kukumakrankas *(see pg 43)* growing in a pot. 'I made some kukumakranka *witblits* once,' she explains, 'and all the old people want it. This is what they remember growing up with. It's good for every sort of ailment!' Kukumakrankas are so rare today that you're lucky if you see them in the *veld* once in your lifetime. It used to be the tradition for men to wear a kukumakranka in the band of their hat, together with a guinea fowl and ostrich feather.'

With traditional values dying out, some of the problems of the city have encroached on these tranquil farms. While Isobel keeps an eye on the past, she and others like her are also keenly aware of the present, and realise that the need for security is essential.

'You've got to be sensible,' she says with a smile. 'But didn't you pass two angels at our gates? They certainly look over us.'

Isobel's waterblommetjiebredie

1–2kg *waterblommetjies*
1kg fatty mutton cut into cubes and rolled in flour
salt
about 2 tablespoons cooking oil
1 big onion, chopped
1 cup of warm water or white wine
a bunch *suring* or oxalis (or juice of half a lemon)
6 potatoes, peeled and cut into pieces
pepper to taste

Break flowers off the stems and soak for a few hours or even overnight in some salt water. Rinse well with cold running water. Shake off any excess water and *goggas*.

Sprinkle salt over the meat. Heat the oil and cook the meat over a low heat until it turns brown. Add the chopped onion and cook until soft. Add the water or wine, put the lid back on and let the meat simmer slowly for about 1½ hours.

Place the *waterblommetjies* and *suring* on top of the lamb. Then add the potatoes. Simmer for about 1 hour until tender. Top up with water if necessary, but don't stir the *bredie* while it is cooking, as the flowers will break. Add a little ground black pepper (*waterblommetjies* have their own pepperiness so taste before you add too much).

Serve with fluffy white rice, sliced beetroot and pickled cucumber.

Hendrik Frieslaar – wood-burning stove restorer

Hendrik Frieslaar is the old stove guy. He lives in Saron, a small missionary station outside Porterville that's definitely seen better days. The church still takes pride of place in the centre of the town nestled under the mountains. It's picturesque but really poor, and there are lots of old folks leaning over their open doors while youngsters stroll the street.

In another lifetime Hendrik would probably have been an engineer. He's a magician with his hands and finds old wrecked wood-burning stoves, which he lovingly restores in record time before selling on. He's got a beat-up old *bakkie* that he uses to drive around the Karoo and Northern Cape, buying up stoves or rescuing them from scrap metal merchants. It's not unheard of for him to pay R25 for a shattered shell of a stove and sell it on for around R1 500. *'Maar hulle is vrek swaar,'* comments this tiny wizened man ('But they are hellishly heavy').

Hendrik's yard looks chaotic but he knows exactly where everything is and could do this work blindfolded. As he talks he runs his hands over the different stoves: there's a Queen Anne, Star Dover, Skotoswede, Welcome Dover, Bolinder, and J. & C.G. Stockholm.

Previous spread Waterblommetjies *grow in abundance on the farm Môrester outside Porterville. Farm matriarch Isobel van Niekerk knows all there is to know about* waterblommetjiebredies, *down to garnishing them with a few sprigs of yellow suring.*

This spread *Hendrik Frieslaar, with his weathered face and warm heart, is the angel of mercy to old stoves, which he rescues off rubbish dumps and lovingly restores before selling them on to eager buyers who can't do without a Welcome Dover.*

The best of the lot is the Dover, says Hendrik, while his wife, Lenie, nods her head in agreement.

'Every home should have a wood-burning stove,' she advises emphatically. She herself doesn't, but she does have her eye on the Ruby standing in the corner of the shed.

'I love anything old,' explains the 70-something Hendrik, who points out the battered grain bins, organs, cupboards and wagon lamps stashed away. An extremely old wheelbarrow that most probably dates to the beginning of the 20th century, with old-fashioned cog and spoke wheels, waits for repair in the yard together with so many other treasures.

'There's never enough time to fix everything,' bemoans Hendrik, who supports a family of children, grandchildren and a foster child. His sons, it seems, show no interest in learning from their self-taught father.

Lui (lazy) Letta, the extremely tame sheep, noses around and comes to look at the latest assortment of stoves that are being repaired. She's just had a lamb that follows her every move, and Letta seems to contribute to the conversation by standing close by and watching Hendrik's every move. 'She's a *huiskind*. You've got to keep an eye on her,' explains Lenie. 'If you forget to close the door, she comes into the kitchen and will eat everything in sight if you aren't careful – coffee, sugar, it doesn't matter!'

'I used to collect buchu when I was young,' says a smiling Hendrik who can remember the day he climbed to the top of Sneeukop and wrote his name on the mountain. For now, he gives new life to old things. But, as with so many other old *Weskussers*, these skills are not being taken up by the next generation.

Favourites

You can't leave the area without:

- **Spending a weekend in Goedverwacht.** A few families open their homes to overnight guests and you'll really get a feel of the village when you wake up with the crowing cocks and head indoors only when the sun leaves the pretty valley. There are two great walks from the village – the Peerboom trail leads from the old graveyard and comes out above Wittewater. Klok se Poort is a tougher route but also really pretty, especially in spring. If you want to drive, take the back route from Goedverwacht to the top of the Piketberg. You'll come to a closed gate on some *omie*'s farm but *gaan maar aan*. Just remember to close the gate behind you.
- **Getting caught up in the excitement of the hang- and paragliding championships** that are held each summer. The usually quiet Dasklip Pass becomes a hive of activity as neon-coloured gliders take to the skies. You might even be inspired to book a tandem flight!
- **Going hiking in the Groot Winterhoek Mountains.** The *fynbos* is spectacular and if you go in January or February you might be lucky to find the gorgeous *Disa uniflora*. There are a number of self-catering cottages in the reserve, which will really allow you to get away from it all.
- **Seeing if you can find somebody to sell you some *herebone*,** a real *Sandveld* speciality. They are big marbled beans that are also known as *goewerneursboontjies* because they were reserved only for the governors or gentlemen. They're delicious simply boiled and served warm with a light vinaigrette dressing.
- **Heading for the crystal pools at Grootfontein Farm** tucked high up in the Olifantsriver Mountains. This private nature reserve is a Natural Heritage Site and the setting is really beautiful. You can camp or stay in rustic cottages at Beaverlac to soak up the peace. Take along a lilo for plenty of pool lolling and dreamy drifting in the cola-coloured water.
- **Spending a weekend on Kersefontein.** It's a working farm but is a perfect place from which to explore the West Coast. In spring the flowers are spectacular and if you have the nerve you might even be able to accompany host Julian Melck on a boar hunt.
- **Driving down Versveld Pass.** While you're admiring the spectacular views, spare a thought for the first farmers who heaved their ox wagons up and down a rudimentary track when they heard the cannon go off to let them know ships had sailed into the harbour at Table Bay.
- **Relaxing with a glass of ice-cold ginger beer** at the Piket-bo-berg Tea Garden. Early spring is also a wonderful time to visit the area when the blossoms are out and the air is perfumed with delicate wafts of peach and plum.
- **Going home with an enormous bunch of spectacular bought proteas.** They'll remind you of the mountains and endless views.
- **Driving past a field of bright yellow canola** and marvelling at what a beautiful country we live in.
- **Buying some wine from Porterville Cellars.** There's no such thing as too much wine or a cellar that is too full.
- **Cycling up Dasklip Pass.** Going up will be hell, but excellent for training. Coming down needs to be done with caution – you don't want to fly off the edge unless you have a back-up parachute!
- **Tucking into a hearty, home-made *waterblommetjiebredie*** with a glass of good local red wine. Delicious. Even better if you're sitting next to a wood-burning stove.
- **Attending a church service at the Hopefield church.** The organ is enormous and the sound rich and mellow.
- **Going for a horse ride** at Excelsior Farm. It's the best way to explore the mountain and you'll be able to smell the *fynbos* as the horses brush past, hear the creak of leather and feel like a kid again.
- **Staying in the sweet self-catering cottages on Tamarak protea farm** and asking Anniza to drop off one of her fantastic meals. You're in for a treat: old fashioned sweet potatoes, home-made chicken pie, salad, courgette bake, and a piping hot dessert with ice-cream that will get delivered by Anniza in the farm *bakkie*. Fantastic, but don't leave this request to the last minute ...
- **Attending the Piketberg flower show** that takes place at the beginning of spring.

Tourism Bureaux

Aurora Tourism: (022) 783-1821

Goedverwacht Tourism: (022) 912-4410

Hopefield Tourism: (022) 715-1142

Koringberg Tourism: (022) 423-8024

Moorreesburg Tourism: (022) 433-1072

Piketberg Tourism: (022) 913-2063

Porterville Tourism: (022) 931-3732

Contact numbers

Disa Tours (mid-Jan to mid-Feb): (022) 931-3732

Excelsior Farm: (022) 914-5853

Goedverwacht hiking trails: (022) 912-4514

Groot Winterhoek Nature Reserve: (022) 931-3732

Hendrik Frieslaar: 076 307 2653, or ask in the village

Paragliding/Hangliding: (022) 931-3416

Piket-bo-berg Tea Garden: (022) 914-5626

Winkelshoek Curio Shop and Farm Stall: (022) 913-1092

Where to stay

Beaverlac: (022) 931-2945

Excelsior Farm: (022) 914-5853

Goedverwacht guest house: (022) 912-4545

Goedverwacht homestay: (022) 912-4410

Gousblom B&B, Aurora: (022) 952-1577

Kersefontein: (022) 783-0850

Langrietvlei: (022) 783-0856

Tamarak Cottages: (022) 914-5600

Wheatfields Country House: (022) 433-2607

This spread *Tender shoots of bright green wheat greet the sun on a farm up the West Coast.*

Mountain majesty

Citrusdal, The Cederberg, Langkloof, Eselbank, Wupperthal, Clanwilliam, Elands Bay, Lambert's Bay

The splendid Cederberg mountain range has drawn people to it for millennia. Its craggy peaks are bursting with fauna and flora that we are only beginning to discover. The first people were the San who made their mythical marks in isolated caves and under rocky overhangs. Then the farmers arrived to make their way in the unforgiving landscape. Today, the mountains and nearby towns attract scores of holidaymakers desperate to soak up the sense of wilderness and solitude.

Citrusdal

The N7 north to Citrusdal is mesmerising. The hills are soft and rolling – a legacy of an age, around 350 million years ago, when this part of the Western Cape would have been under water. There are more than a few hills named Rondeberg or Rondeheuwel meaning 'round hill' and it's not impossible to imagine them in a seascape of waves.

Today it's the breeze in the knee-high wheat, rye and barley that causes waves to ripple over the surface. It's an emerald green world now, but come the end of summer when the grain is harvested, the land will look parched and bleached and not for the faint-hearted. You'll pass a farm called Somersverdriet or 'Summer's Sadness'. The name says it all.

Slow down and you're likely to see tufts of wool caught on the barbed wire fence, or the huge brown flanks of cows lying in a field of verdant freshness, chewing the cud and idly swishing flies away. There's a whitewashed barn with enormous red doors and a sagging roof. It's a typical South African scene; these images are branded into our subconscious somewhere, never to be erased.

And then, just when you begin to tire of the sameness of the farms, and have finished all the dried peaches and *droëwors* you had packed for *padkos*, the mountains appear like a prehistoric beast strutting across the wide landscape. It's up over Piekenierskloof with the views over the Swartland to your left, and then down into Citrusdal situated on the bank of the Oliphants River.

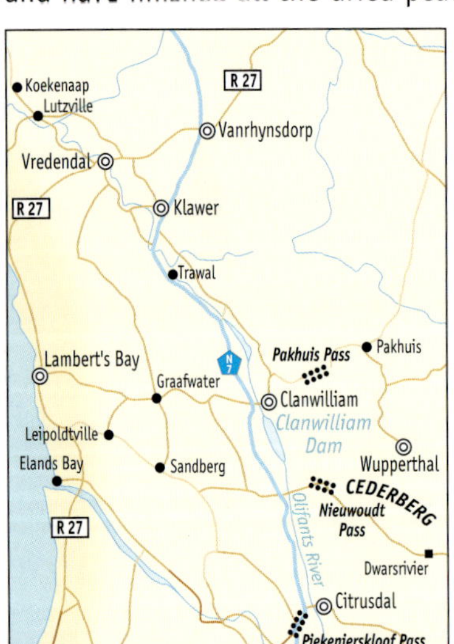

There was a time, not that long ago really, when this valley wasn't filled with neat citrus farms. It teemed with game – eland and other antelope, lion and, of course, elephant, from which the river got its name. There are records dating from 1660 in which explorers report seeing 200 to 300 elephants in a day on the banks of the river.

The simple museum in the town, situated in an old sandstone church, is an interesting reminder of the olden days. There's Anglo-Boer War memorabilia, rudimentary farming implements and things that have absolutely no bearing on our lives today. It's a poignant tribute to how quickly things change and how, one day, our descendants could rummage through our precious household items exclaiming, 'What on earth is this?' while handling objects we can't imagine living without.

The real joy of Citrusdal is discovered from early spring when the first orange blossoms open and the air is perfumed with the smell of neroli. It's intoxicating – warm, sensual and evocative. In winter, when the blossoms have given way to bright orange fruit, the trees are laden with oranges, naartjies and clementines.

But there's more to Citrusdal than just fruit. It's also home to a hot spring that has been popular for centuries. Known simply as The Baths, it's situated in a well-signposted wooded *kloof* at the head of a valley a short distance out of town.

About 15km away from the spring, in the overgrown graveyard at Craig Royston's farm stall there's an assortment of graves. Some have impressive caskets above the ground, while others are just marked by stones. There's a thick covering of moss on the gravestones and the yard is overgrown with a tumble of grass and spring flowers. The site, no doubt, was chosen with care and offers a sweeping view over the valley and onto the Cederberg mountain range.

Previous spread *Sunset on the Piekenierskloof Pass is a moody affair. The climb up the mountain is long and winding, the view from the top over the wheat farms is spectacular, and the descent into Citrusdal is magical, especially in spring when the orange blossoms are out. The Cederberg is home to wonderful wild flowers, also most visible in spring.*

This spread *Citrusdal is named after the fruit that does so well in the valley. In winter bags of clementines and oranges line the side of the road, ready for customers.*

In amongst the greenness are the graves that mark the final resting place of James McGregor (1830–1914) and his wife, Helena (1851–1912), 21 years his junior. Not far from these are another two headstones marking the graves of James Campbell McGregor (died 20 October 1918) with the inscription, 'Until the day break' and William McGregor (died 26 October 1918); the inscription on his grave is 'Rest in Peace'. The two brothers died just six days apart.

The history of The Baths and the McGregor family is intrinsically linked and in 2003, to commemorate the 100 years that The Baths had been in the McGregor family, Hazel Hall wrote the fascinating, *Taking the Waters – The History of the Olifants River Warm Baths, Western Cape*.

This spread *The Cederberg's red-hued rocks are most unforgettable at sunrise or sunset, when the majesty of the mountain is most obvious. Soak up the silence, and look out for Venus, the evening star.*

Long before the Cape was colonised by European settlers, the San had been using the hot spring as a gathering place as they moved between the mountains and the sea. There are San rock paintings near The Baths and as Hazel explains, 'The physical and spiritual worlds of the San were so intertwined, they would almost certainly have harnessed supernatural power from the hot water for healing purposes.'

The first mention of The Baths was made obliquely in 1739 when an official of the Dutch East India Company recommended that two military outposts be built – one near Klawer and the other '*aan ter Warme Bad*' or 'at the Warm Baths'. After that the baths changed hands a number of times and were alternately cared for or left to wrack and ruin.

The Baths were sold to a syndicate that had grand plans for it, which included the building of a tunnel through the mountains to create a railway connection to Porterville. But the Anglo-Boer War

(1899–1902) put paid to these ideas and, in 1903, James McGregor from Modderfontein farm (where Craig Royston now is) took ownership and set about making significant changes.

By all accounts James McGregor was a remarkable man. A description in Hazel's book sums up his true grit. After emigrating from Scotland to South Africa, the young James set off to Australia to see if he could make his fortune during the gold rush. 'After about six years of fluctuating fortune, James McGregor decided to return to South Africa, quite possibly because he was homesick for his family.

He arrived by ship in East London and because the next vessel headed for Cape Town would not pass by for a further two months, he decided to walk the distance. The first day out, a cart bound for the Cape passed by, but the occupants refused to give him a lift. That night he passed the cart as he walked and each day the cart passed him later and later until he left it behind altogether. He probably averaged about 55km a day – which would have meant three weeks of walking – and arrived quite unexpectedly at his home in Maitland, a grown man who had gone away a little boy.'

Even in matters of the heart, James was unstoppable. 'James met and fell in love with the beautiful Helena (Lenie) Jacoba van Wyk, a tall and imposing woman who towered over the stocky James McGregor,' writes Hazel. 'The courtship, however, must have been quite difficult for the young man, as Lenie's parents did not take kindly to *uitlanders*,' which is exactly what James would have been as a Scotsman and a new import to the valley. 'The Van Wyks lived at Kanolvlei (over the Pakhuis Pass) near Clanwilliam and had been resident in the district since at least 1739. When James went there to trade, he was not allowed into the house. But of course true love won in the end – although only after promising in his marriage vows that he would never take her to his foreign land, there over the sea.'

A combination of hard work and ingenuity made James a wealthy man and in 1903 he bought The Baths. With the help of his three sons, he built good roads, an elegant, balconied guesthouse and several fine stone bath-houses, some of which are still there today. Tragedy struck in 1918 when the two younger sons, William and James, died in the Spanish flu epidemic. However, The Baths ended up in the hands of their seven sisters, who were just as hardworking and efficient as their father.

In Hazel's book there's a lovely sepia photo of the McGregor sisters. There's a quiet confidence about them as they look directly into the camera and out into the world. Though each woman has a story to tell, Florrie's is the most poignant.

'Grace Florence McGregor, born 19 September 1893, was the baby of the family, and she bore a striking resemblance to Princess Elizabeth (now Queen Elizabeth II). In fact, she was once mistaken for the Princess in Cape Town. Florrie, however, led a rather unhappy life,' writes Hazel.

'She was in love with three men at different times, two of whom she was actually engaged to. The first was John Ness, who had a farm in Nyasaland (now Malawi) to which he wanted to take Florrie. John was asked to farm, instead, at Modderfontein, but he refused so the engagement ended. Then Trygve Morch Olsen came along, and Florrie became engaged to him and was getting her trousseau ready for her future with him when he ran off with her sister Lizzie. This must have been a great disappointment to her.

'Her third love was Harry Hall. After Trygve and Lizzie had moved to Valhalla, Florrie moved with her sister Edie to The Baths. By this time, Harry was already living there. Unhappily for her, Harry – 22 years Florrie's junior – married her niece Margaret Peter. Harry's marriage to Margaret was very distressing for Florrie, and she died a few months later on 23 December 1949 at Arlington Court in Muizenberg. Some say she died of a broken heart. She did die of heart failure, but it was more likely from the consequences of an earlier bout of typhoid fever.'

Today The Baths are a superb family retreat and are a refreshing mixture of the old and new. There's plenty of accommodation in self-catering chalets, at the camping site for those who prefer to be tucked away to do their own thing, or in self-contained flats in the beautiful old Victorian building that presides over the whole complex.

This is the kind of place where, as a child, you spend so long in the water that you come out with wrinkled 'granny fingers' and fall into bed absolutely exhausted at the end of every day. And, as if lolling around in the warm water isn't enough of an attraction, there are tennis courts and hiking trails to keep you busy.

As a day visitor, you can also experience some of The Baths' magic, but only if it isn't full. Wisely, the owners limit the number of visitors every day so that there is always a quiet spot to be found.

The Cederberg

Which adjectives do the Cederberg justice? While rugged, spectacular, craggy and dramatic go part of the way, they fail to capture the majesty of the peaks, the change of light as it hits a rock formation or the smell of *fynbos* as you brush past.

A World Heritage Site

CapeNature is the authority charged with managing this magnificent area with an intriguing history:

- The mountain range is made up mainly of Table Mountain sandstone, which accounts for some of the fantastical shapes, such as the Maltese Cross or the Wolfberg Arch.
- The San and Khoi inhabited the area from the earliest of times. The prolific rock art is all the evidence we need to understand that European settlers weren't the first people drawn to the area or impressed by its beauty and isolation.
- European settlers started stock farming in the area in the early 1700s, and in 1876 a forestry station was established at what is now known as Algeria. It was so named because the Frenchman who was in charge of state forests at that time said that the mountains and the cedar trees reminded him of the Atlas Mountains in Algeria.
- Our forefathers had little regard for the destruction they wrought, and chopped down the cedar trees in epic proportions. The wood was used for furniture and, more mundanely, over 7 000 trees were cut down and used as telephone poles between Piketberg and Calvinia. Cedar trees are now on the brink of extinction.
- The Cederberg is home to a wide range of mammals, reptiles, birds and fish. Probably provoking the most controversy is the leopard. There are some interesting species to be found here and, although they don't have the 'wow!' factor a leopard has, they're important. These include the spectacled dormouse and the armadillo lizard, which is endemic to the area. The Clanwilliam yellow fish, the Clanwilliam red fin minnow and the fired red fin minnow are threatened although other endemic species also face extinction.
- The Cederberg was proclaimed a wilderness area in 1973. CapeNature works in close conjunction with the farmers in the area who are justifiably proud of the conservancy they've helped establish.

Previous spread *Follow the dusty road to Mount Ceder where you'll want to put your feet up for a few days or swim in the refreshing Groot Rivier that runs past the cottages.*

This spread *The orange rocks of the Cederberg strike a dramatic pose.*

Following spread *The Stadsaal (or City Hall) is one of the Cederberg's well-known caves and is rich in San rock art, along with some interesting historical graffiti. Cairns mark the way to the Wolfberg Arch, another Cederberg favourite.*

Cederberg Cellars

Oom Pollie Nieuwoudt was a visionary. You would have to be to plant vines in a place as wild and untamed as the Cederberg. This is not soft farming country. It's hot and dry in summer; in winter, snow regularly blankets the landscape in quiet whiteness. But the Cederberg is also Nieuwoudt country – five generations' worth. As you wind and bump your way up Nieuwoudt Pass, just about every farm signpost carries a Nieuwoudt name. There's Pip at Kromrivier, Jannie at Vogelfontein and Jannie at Jamaka. But it's at Dwarsrivier that you'll find the father and son team, Ernst and David Nieuwoudt, and all the wine action.

It's a Saturday afternoon and David, the winemaker, is on a roll. The mobile bottling plant is parked behind the cellar, there's music blaring from the radio and friends and family are hard at work, or sitting in the sun and enjoying the new Sauvignon Blanc. They're bottling Cederberg Private Cellar's first-ever sparkling wine and David's on a high. So he should be. Together with his father, Ernst, David has played an integral part in establishing the family vineyard as one of the best in the country.

'Ag, it's stunning up here,' says David with an enormous smile. He's dressed in jeans, a trendy shirt and fur-lined green gumboots. 'Everybody laughed when my *oupa* planted the first table grapes in 1965. These were sheep and tobacco farmers so they thought he was crazy. But it's perfect wine country and comparable to places in Chile, which also produces excellent wines.'

Oom Pollie planted the first grapes in the early 1970s and then started making his own wine out of desperation as the co-operative cellar in the area wasn't keen to take his grapes because they came in later than everybody else's. So he decided to go it alone and in 1977 he entered a Cabernet Sauvignon into the SA Young Wine Show. It won the best red wine on show. The farm is 5 500ha and initially 23ha was under vines. This has expanded and they now farm 52ha of grapes.

Asked whether he is planning to plant more, David shakes his head with an emphatic 'No! The Cederberg is one of the most efficiently run and strictly controlled conservancies in the country. If you want to clear five metres of land, you have to submit a document 50cm thick. I think we have enough premium vineyards and we are rather concentrating on the wines.

'The Cederberg climate also means that we harvest extremely healthy fruit. There's no humidity up here so, while we have to spray for powdery mildew, we aren't affected by downy mildew and mealy bug, which can cause havoc in other vineyards.'

Ask him about the soil and he really gets misty-eyed. 'The soils here are stunning,' he says. 'We've got shale and slate, deep red Hutton and Glen Rosa. It imparts a wonderful flintiness to the grapes.'

While David is out there winning awards (just about every wine has a gold or double gold Veritas sticker on it) he's modest about his achievements. 'My dad is the real farmer,' he says quickly. 'He's seen all the changes from tobacco through to fruit and now wine.'

But the Nieuwoudts (which, quite appropriately, means 'new wood') aren't just making inroads into the wine business. They play an integral part in the conservancy and are keen to ensure that the natural legacy they've inherited will remain unspoilt for future generations.

To quote one of David's favourite expressions: 'Ag, stunning!'

Previous spread *Winter bites hard in the Cederberg and frost lies thick on the ground. The Maltese Cross has always enthralled hikers with its spiritual majesty.*

This spread *Cederberg Cellars is one of the highest vineyards in the country. The soil and climate are unique, which adds to the wine's character.*

Ag, it's stunning up here

The Cederberg Observatory

There's something both epic and intimate about a winter slide-show experience at the Cederberg Observatory, latitude 32°29'S, longitude 19°15'E, on Dwarsrivier Farm. Epic because you have the mind-blowing opportunity of looking at stars many light years away. Intimate because, on a beautiful clear night that's perfect for stargazing, the temperatures will drop to around 1°C and you'll probably be preoccupied about whether or not your toes will fall off.

The Cederberg Observatory is owned and run by a group of seven amateur astronomers: eccentric, clever, driven and just a bit batty. But this is exactly what makes them so interesting, and so entertaining. To share their passion – and spread their enthusiasm – they hold a slide-show every Saturday night, except on or near the full moon. The show is a dizzying affair. There's talk of billions of stars in our galaxy and a similar number of galaxies in the universe. Red giants, double stars, black holes, comets, asteroids and planets are mentioned. A planet with a temperature of 300°C and deep space with a temperature approaching -273°C – the mind boggles!

The highlight of the evening, however, has to be a glimpse of the inky skies directly above you. On a clear winter's night when your breath comes out white and billowy, there are parts of the night sky that look close enough to touch.

You'll never find a sky like this in the city. There's too much light pollution and too many other things floating around in the atmosphere that will afford you only a dim display. But up here in the crystal clear Cederberg it's an entirely different story. What's more, you'll have the help of one of the phenomenal telescopes that have been built by Chris Forder, one of the members, who has been passionate about astronomy and telescope making since he was a youngster.

'When we were kids, someone lent a friend and me a telescope and we were lucky enough to watch Saturn rise just after sunset, and then set the following morning just before sunrise. It was a life-changing experience,' explains Chris. 'When the telescope owner moved away and took his instrument with him, we were lost. It was then that we decided to learn to build our own. I made my first telescope back in 1958 and have been making them ever since.'

It takes Chris anything between six months and a year to build one of his massive telescopes, which he names. Two at the observatory are known fondly as Bertha and Bertie. 'But you've got to watch out for aperture fever. In astronomy, size definitely counts!' he laughs.

'The bigger the telescope, the greater your aperture, which means you can let in more light. The end result is that you see more and that's very compelling. When I get bored with a telescope, I get rid of it and start working on the next one.'

One of Chris's most memorable astronomical experiences happened at the beginning of 2005. 'Sometimes we sleep outside under the stars,' he explains with the infectious enthusiasm of a child. 'I woke up because I thought somebody was flashing a torch in my face. Instead it was this enormous fireball moving across the sky. It was incredible

eccentric, clever, driven and just a bit batty

and gave off more light than the moon does. Thankfully, earth is surrounded by atmosphere; otherwise that would have left a rather large crater when it hit terra firma!'

'Stargazing is a humbling experience,' says another of the partners. 'We have a small idea of just how many galaxies there are and what's going on out there, and that really brings you down to earth. We accept more now, knowing what we do about the stars. Whatever is going to happen, will happen and there's no point fretting needlessly. As a result, we're a fairly laid-back group. What will be will be, and we have no power to change the course of the universe!'

Matjiesrivier Cedar Nursery

Rika du Plessis has the patience of a saint – or at least comes close. As the CapeNature's conservation manager at Matjiesrivier Nature Reserve, where the Cederberg's cedar nursery is situated, she's responsible for growing cedar tree saplings and then replanting them when they're big enough to withstand the rigours of the extremes in Cederberg weather – the heat in summer and then freezing temperatures in winter.

It's not an easy job. The Clanwilliam cedar tree (*Widdringtonia cedarbergensis*) is a slow-growing species and can't be rushed. The survival rate of nursery-propagated saplings is also pitiful, which makes Rika's job all the more challenging. The Cederberg is named after the cedar tree and yet, over the centuries, we've shown it so little respect. Except, thankfully, for now. This handsome species grows either dead straight, which explains why it was so popular for telephone poles, or into fantastical, gnarled shapes, and is found at an altitude of between 1 000 and 1 700m. The wood is heavily perfumed and durable, perfect for furniture, which is why it was harvested so heavily in the 19th and early 20th centuries.

Apart from people, the cedar's other major enemy is fire. When flames raced across the mountains in the blistering summer of 2000, one of the last remaining cedar plantations was all but completely burnt out. A few trees survived and it's hoped that the plantation will regenerate itself.

Now, in an attempt to reverse the de-forestation and prevent the tree from facing extinction, people like Rika are working at cultivating saplings that can then be replanted in the *veld*.

She explains how they go about collecting the seeds in lyrical sounding places such as Sneeuberg, Krakadouw, Sneeukop, and Heuningvlei. 'Cedar trees are so closely protected that even we need to apply for a permit for permission to collect seeds.

'We head out in summer to the different areas where trees are still

Previous spread *Pink paper flowers add colour to the stark winter landscape when the vines at Cederberg Cellars lie dormant, waiting for the first warmth of spring. An abandoned building at Matjiesrivier speaks of hard times in a punishing environment.*

This spread *The Cederberg Observatory, where you will be treated to a whistle-stop introduction to the night skies, is fun for young and old visitors. In winter you'll want to dress up warmly as the temperature plummets on crystal clear nights.*

fantastical, gnarled shapes

growing and collect the cones that are beginning to open. It's these seeds that are mature enough for germination.

'You get 12 seeds from each cone,' Rika continues, 'so we don't collect every year because we usually have enough and we also want to leave seeds so they're able to germinate naturally. The cones are then stored at room temperature and as they dry the four scales pull apart and the seeds inside are released.

'This project has been going for two years and everything we do is very carefully monitored,' Rika clarifies. 'We keep the trees from different areas separate, and we record how each tree was propagated. We only plant trees back in the area they originated from. There's a study proposal to investigate if there are genetic differences between the trees, but until we know for sure we are keeping them apart just to be safe.'

It's a formidable job that involves plenty of trailblazing and thinking on your feet. 'Initially we were planting out the saplings when they were a year old, but the survival rate was low so now we're keeping them for two years to see if that makes a difference,' she says hopefully.

Once the saplings are planted, GPS co-ordinates are taken so that the tree can be monitored. Even if the trees survive the first few years and there's no big fire, progress is still slow.

'Cedar trees only become sexually mature and produce seed at around 25 to 30 years so we've got a long way to go,' Rika continues.

Will she be around that long to see the fruits of her hard labour?

'I certainly hope so!' she says with determination. And you get the feeling from Rika that that means yes, without any doubt.

Stay and play

The Cederberg Wilderness Reserve and nearby Matjiesriver Nature Reserve make up more than 80 000ha of natural splendour and both are designated wilderness areas. There are plenty of places to stay in the Cederberg and, if you like camping, this is the place to head to.

- CapeNature has campsites along the Rondegat River at **Algeria** as well as a number of self-catering chalets. The Kliphuis campsite is on the Pakhuis Pass on the flower route to the Biedouw Valley and Wupperthal. Call (022) 931-2088/2900 or visit www.capenature.org.za
- **Sanddrif** on the farm Dwarsrivier offers self-catering cottages and camping. Particularly popular among hikers, climbers and mountain bikers, it's near the Maltese Cross and the Wolfberg Arch as well as the Cederberg Observatory. Call (027) 482-2825.
- **Sevilla and Traveller's Rest**, on the other side of the Pakhuis Pass, have self-catering accommodation. Visit during flower season when their restaurant, Khoisan Kitchen, is open. Call (027) 482-1824.
- **Mount Ceder** in the southern Cederberg is an absolute gem and has lovely cottages, a restaurant and conference centre on the Grootrivier. Call (023) 317-0848 or visit www.mountceder.co.za
- Stay in stylish strawbale cottages and experience the thrill of whitewater paddling during winter at **Oudrif**. Call (027) 482-2397 or visit www.oudrif.co.za

This spread *The area is named after the Cedar trees that used to cover the mountains. Over-harvesting and fire have, unfortunately, taken their toll.*

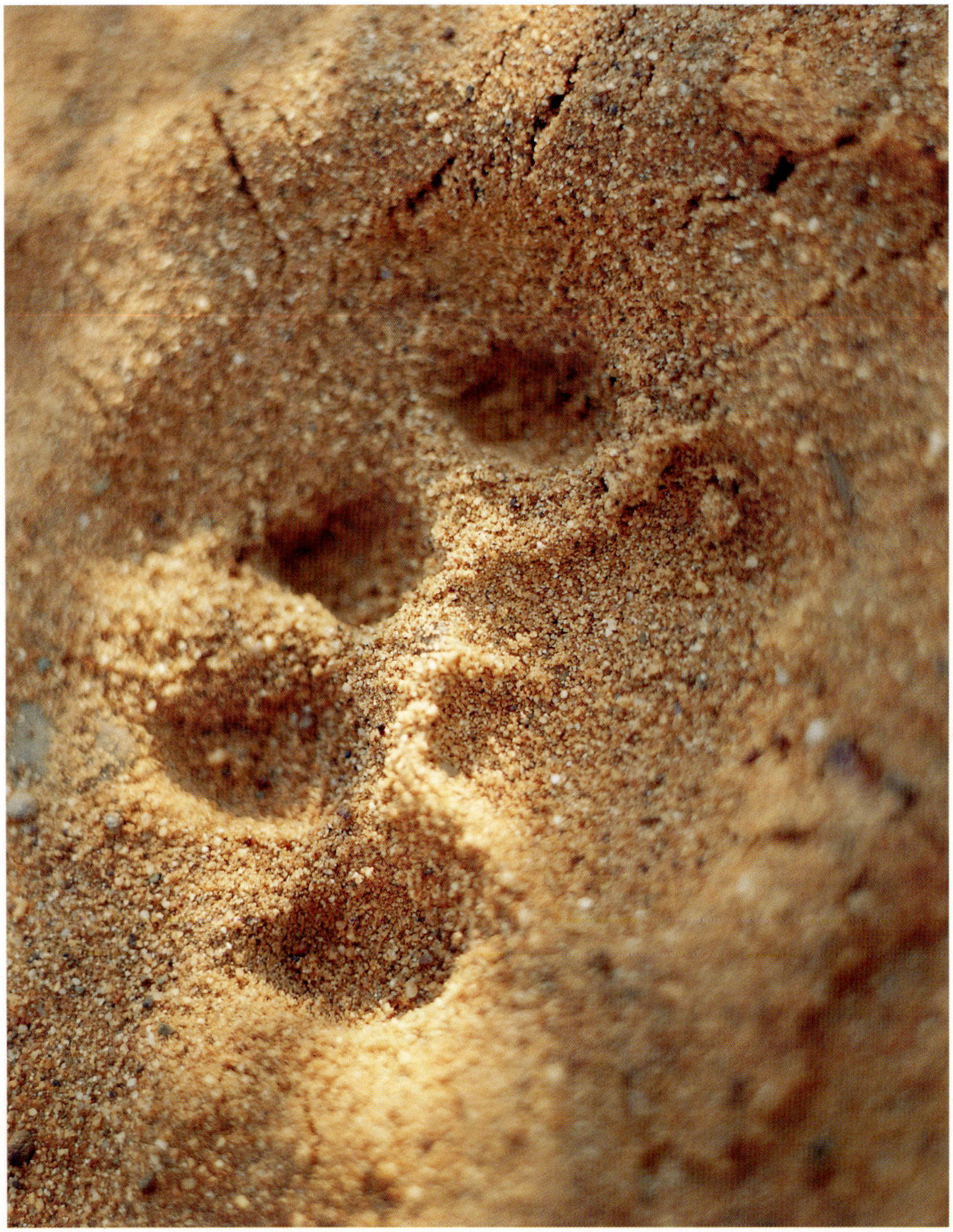

The Cape Leopard Trust

There's always public outrage when there's a report of a leopard caught in a gin trap. Rightly so! Any animal caught in this way faces a slow and agonising death – especially if the traps are not checked every day.

However, on the other side of the argument, if you're a stock farmer and a leopard kills 30 sheep in one night, what are you to do? Researchers Quinton and Nicole Martins, in conjunction with the farmers who live in the Cederberg, are hoping to come up with a solution.

Realising just how vulnerable these big cats are, they established The Cape Leopard Trust in 2003. The aim of their study is to gain an understanding of the ecology of the leopards in this area – sex ratios, densities, home ranges and more. All this information will make it easier to implement effective management strategies and hopefully promote greater understanding and buy-in from farmers who are tempted to set traps to keep the predators at bay.

While gin traps are old-fashioned and look as though they date back to some Medieval torture chamber, Quinton and Nicole's equipment is high-tech and sophisticated. They have set up a series of cameras, which are movement-activated, on either side of the track that leopards are known to use. So far, they have had some rewarding sightings and are beginning to understand the animals' habits. To date, they have been able to identify 12 different leopards in the area on the eastern side of the wilderness that ranges from Wupperthal in the north to Grootrivier in the south.

An added, and unexpected, benefit of the leopard cameras is that other animals have been caught on film. The list is long and includes aardwolf, aardvark, African wildcat, Cape mountain zebra, honey badger, porcupine, mongoose and a variety of small antelopes.

Quinton goes on to explain the role that leopards play. 'Leopards are the apex predator in the Western Cape. Leopards are also "sexy" animals to work on and this allows us to draw in valuable resources, which can also be used in protecting smaller, lower profile species such as caracal and jackal.

'Unfortunately, leopards have suffered on a number of fronts. They have lost territory to farming and development and have been killed in areas where they've had a negative impact on local farmers. Today, the long-term survival of leopards rests on their densities within protected areas. As such, reliable population estimates are essential for effective conservation management.'

But farmers need more than just academic research or outrage to encourage them to change their ways. 'You've got to provide somebody with a solution,' says Quinton. 'Or at least a half-way solution!'

For The Cape Leopard Trust, one of the answers might lie in the introduction of Anatolian Shepherds – dogs that are bred to bond with sheep and act as their protectors. These dogs, also known as the Anatolian Karabash, originated in Turkey on the Anatolian plains where sheep are raised in their thousands.

'Farmers in Namibia have had fantastic success with these dogs,' says Quinton, 'and so we are donating young pups to certain farmers in the Cederberg to help them manage their stock losses.

'Good news stories are always great and I was chatting to a farmer in Namibia who told me that he used to kill several hundred predators a year to curb stock losses. He would put down poison, set traps, put poison collars on his lambs – the works. But, despite his efforts, his stock losses didn't diminish. Then he introduced Anatolian Shepherds onto his farm and he hasn't had a single loss since then.

'It's not a cure-all. The dogs need to be well trained and managed so you have to proceed cautiously. But, so far, it's looking good,' ends Quinton as he heads out the door.

The call of the spoor proves just too strong after all!

This spread *Caught on camera! The Cape Leopard Trust is dedicated to helping track leopards in the Cederberg – and other animals also get a show-in.*

Langkloof

This small settlement, on the bumpy jeep track from Matjiesrivier to Wupperthal, is hard to get to and easy to bypass. The track is fit only for donkeys and sheep, really, and then near Moordenaarsgat (Murderer's Valley) you take a left-hand turn and head towards the base of Tafelberg, which towers overhead.

The tiny community of roughly 15 families is an outpost of the bigger Moravian Mission Station at Wupperthal. There are around six such villages in the Cederberg, established on land that's still owned by the church.

Oom Piet Salomo is the man to visit in Langkloof. He's 80 years old and, when he's not at church, he's busy working under the old oak tree in his yard making boxes out of the fragrant cedar trees he finds on the mountain. The old man is small and more than a little bent – much like the trees that grow on these craggy peaks. But he's got a warm smile and a firm handshake.

He has been working with wood for decades and makes boxes to order, and also to sell in the shop at Dwarsrivier, where his grandson Mark works with David Nieuwoudt at Cederberg Cellar.

'A big toy box takes about a week to finish,' he says. 'You can see this one has got the holes made by a wasp that made its nest in the tree. But the customer doesn't want me to cover up the blemish. He says it gives the box character, *gees*. I've got to make a matching pair. But getting the wood isn't easy. My legs are starting to feel as though they belong to a much older man and I can't climb the mountain like I used to. And you can't just take any wood. You need a permit and you can only take trees that have been burnt or fallen down. Then you've got to cut it and let it dry for a couple of months before you can use it for furniture.'

The smell from the shavings surrounding the work area is wonderful and makes you want to scoop up handfuls and bury your nose in it. It's a smell that is reminiscent of pine, resin, wood oil, rocks and mountain streams. 'We love the smell, but moths hate it,' explains Oom Piet. 'It's an insect repellent. That's why it was so popular for cupboards.'

'We are Salomo,' he explains carefully. 'In the Cape that's Solomons, but we're different here in Langkloof.'

This spread *A visit to Oom Piet Salomo at the small settlement of Langkloof is a treat. He's strictly old school and believes in good, honest work with his hands. His fragrant, hand-crafted cedar boxes are well worth investing in.*

Following spread *A young girl in Eselbank shares her lunch with two furry friends. The village is about 13km from Wupperthal on a bumpy jeep track.*

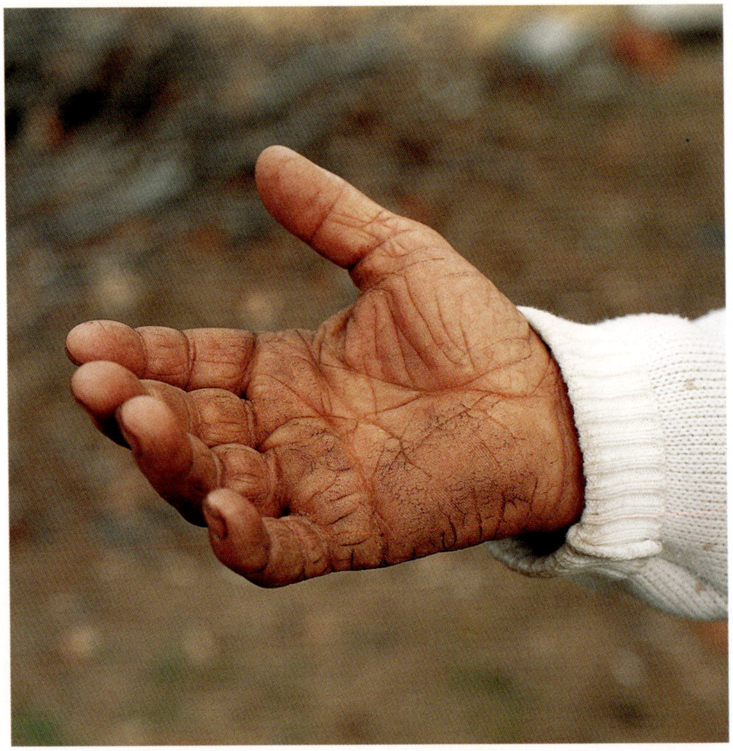

Eselbank

About 13km from Wupperthal, Eselbank is another village that looks as though it comes from a different time when the pace was slower and people had plenty of time to *kuier*. Park your car, and pretty soon you'll be joined by a variety of residents wanting to pass the time of day and find out what draws you to this neck of the woods.

If you're lucky, D.C. Mouton might swing by with his walking stick in one gnarled hand and a bagful of stories slung over his shoulder. His initials D.C. stand for Dirk Cornelius and he has a silver tongue and a ready laugh. He's also wearing well-worn and well-oiled *velskoene* from Clanwilliam – the mark of a real local.

Roughly translated, Eselbank means 'donkey ridge or bank' and hints at just how much a part of life these humble – and sometimes stubborn – animals are. They're used to work the fields and also as a means of transport. Although there are more cars now than ever before in the village, for years getting anywhere meant hitching up the donkey *karretjie* and hoping that the little furry grey animals with the strange marking of the cross on their backs were feeling strong and, more importantly, obedient.

For now, though, the donkeys are having a holiday. Jean Mouton, another chatty resident, explains that the donkeys are walked over the mountains in an easterly direction and turned loose to graze and rest before the hard work during spring and summer begins again.

This spread *Every village has its characters and Eselbank is no exception. D.C. Mouton has calloused hands, a warm heart and plenty of stories up his sleeve. The treat is in the telling when his eyes light up and his sense of humour surfaces.*

'In the olden days we used to span in 16 donkeys at a time,' explains D.C. 'Now mostly we work with less. We usually put three in front, one in the middle and two behind. The strong ones go in the front, but you also have to choose the leaders carefully otherwise they'll just push off in any direction that they like while you're left dragging behind shouting, "whoa! whoa!"

'There are some donkeys that learn quickly and then there are others that are far too independent,' he continues, demonstrating in brilliant mime what you look like when you're being taken on an unscheduled donkey ride. Next, with his *'baie gemaklike' velskoene* flashing, he does a couple of deft manoeuvres and dance steps to show what happens if he encounters a snake in the fields.

But back to the donkeys. Choosing names for each animal when there's a huge herd poses some challenges, but D.C. reels off just a few to start. There's Geelbek, Knoppie, Rhebok, Springbok and Duiker.

For all their recalcitrance and legendary stubbornness, donkeys are also hardy and do well under hard conditions. What's more, they're not just farmhands – there are reports of them acting as great shepherds to flocks of sheep, braying madly if any dogs (both wild and domesticated) come close to a flock they've bonded with.

When D.C. has exhausted his donkey stories, he moves on to talking about life in his small village. It's peaceful, there's no crime and they get by. Getting into town is a bit of a mission – they go to Wupperthal for basics but then head to the bright lights of *Klam*william when they want to do a bigger shop or are looking for goods at better prices.

'Why Klam(damp)william?' one asks stupidly.

'You can buy alcohol there,' laughs D.C. – it being something not so easy to come by in the Moravian village of Wupperthal.

There's a clay oven next to the main road. It was built by Jean Mouton (of course he and D.C. are related) and is used by Ansie Mouton who lives over the road and is married to Jean's brother. It's a stone and clay affair, the mouth of the oven blackened from years of use, around 30 years old; and has seen more than a few loaves of bread. It's easy to use: you light a fire in the oven, allow it to heat up and then scoop out the coals carefully before sliding in your baking tins. Then you close the mouth of the oven with a simple sheet of iron and prop it shut with whatever is lying nearby.

Ansie's bread recipe has remained unchanged – much like life in the village. It's made using potato as the starter, or leaven, and produces impressive, healthy looking loaves.

'I bake a couple of times a week,' says Ansie quietly. 'Tourists passing through often want to buy my bread so I sell it for around R12 a loaf.' Ansie is unsure how long it takes for the bread to cook. 'You've just got to look at it,' says the unassuming expert who could probably do all this in her sleep.

One of Ansie's favourite recipes is for crisp apricot biscuits *(see below)*. Interestingly they are very similar to the biscuits made by generations of women who lived at Ganzekraal on the West Coast, only they add generous amounts of ginger, cinnamon and cloves. Ansie reckons they're good with a cup of tea, while at Ganzekraal they thought their biscuits were good on picnics and 'excellent served with brandy after hunting'.

Ansie's apricot biscuits

12 cups flour
1 tablespoon bicarbonate of soda
6 cups brown sugar
500g butter
6 eggs
2 cups smooth apricot jam

Mix flour, bicarbonate of soda and sugar together. Rub in butter. Beat eggs with jam and add to the mixture. If it's too stiff add a little water. Roll out and cut with cookie cutters. Or roll into little balls and push them flat with a fork. Bake for about 10–15 minutes in a hottish oven until golden brown.

This spread *The jeep track from Matjiesrivier to Wupperthal is bumpy, but it's worth any bone jarring. Along the way you'll pass settlements such as Langkloof and Eselbank where you can stop to buy Ansie Mouton's fresh bread or biscuits.*

a stone and clay affair

Rooibos

Love it or hate it, rooibos (*Aspalathus linearis*) is as much a part of this region as rock art, *velskoen* and stunning spring flowers. There are more than 200 species of *Aspalathus* (of the legume family) found in South Africa, but rooibos is the only species that's extensively farmed and harvested. And, if it hadn't been for the local inhabitants who have been using the bruised leaves as a beverage for centuries, there's a good chance that this 'mountain tea' would never have been discovered. Today, however, it's a huge and lucrative business and rooibos is exported around the world.

This humble tea made headlines in June 2005 when a lengthy lawsuit in America around the rooibos trademark was finally settled. Simply, a U.S. company attempted to secure the name 'rooibos' as a trademark, which would have meant that the tea grown and produced on local soils wouldn't have been able to use the name we all grew up with. This was eventually thrown out of court because, the judges believed, the name rooibos was a generic word used to describe tea and couldn't be secured as a trademark.

Its health properties are well known. Rooibos is caffeine-free, anti-spasmodic, relieves allergies, is rich in anti-oxidants, increases iron absorption and contains a number of essential minerals. It's good for drinking, useful in cooking, and now many bodycare products also contain rooibos extracts.

Although *Aspalathus linearis* is indigenous, the seeds are hard to come by. This is because each legume produces only one seed, popping open and shooting it out when it's ripe. Finding these tiny seeds in the sand is eye-straining work and farmers have to sift the sand around the plants. However, ants also harvest the rooibos seeds, so anthills are often good seed reservoirs to be plundered by farmers.

One kilogram of seed will produce about eight hectares of rooibos. As if finding them isn't difficult enough, the seeds also have a really hard shell that makes germination tricky. Today, the seeds are mechanically scrubbed to help break down the hard shell, which more than doubles the seeds' germination potential.

an ancient way to travel

Wupperthal

Wupperthal is everything you would expect from an old mission station. Founded in 1830, the village has a sense of peace and purpose, which is emphasised by the solid whitewash-and-thatch buildings. There are echoes of this village in other mission stations such as Elim in the Overberg, Genadendal near Greyton, and Mamre close to Darling.

On a late Sunday afternoon Wupperthal is bathed in a somnambulant air. Children play in the streets with higgledy-piggledy home-made go-carts while adults in their Sunday best stand by their gates watching the not-too-hectic world go by.

The mission station was established by the Rev. Johann Gottlieb Leipoldt and Baron Theobald von Wurmb of the Rhenish Missionary Society on a farm originally known as Rietmond next to the Tra-Tra River.

Mission stations such as these occupy an uneasy place in South African history. In anticipation of the abolition of slavery in 1834, the British government at the Cape adopted a hard line policy towards freed slaves and the remaining nomadic Khoekhoe clans. Under these laws, all Khoekhoen or 'free blacks' as they were known, without a fixed abode, were liable to be forced into farm labour. Given the dire conditions on many of the farms, the mission stations, which provided access to land in return for conversion to Christianity, quickly became attractive alternatives and it's hardly surprising that the they expanded quickly.

For many, a fairly cynical conversion to Christianity was the only way to avoid a gruelling life of hard labour. Moreover, although mission station rules were often very strict, they did provide an excellent education and the opportunity to work and gain valuable skills. Not surprisingly, the mission stations throughout the Cape often ran foul of local farmers and the authorities. Many farmers were largely illiterate and became increasingly unhappy about the idea of an educated and skilled underclass.

However, for people used to being on the move and in tune with living close to the ebb and flow of nature, the rules must have seemed overwhelming and more than stifling at times. These regulations included obligatory daily church attendance, the holding of no other beliefs, no magic, swearing, or misuse of the name of God.

No alcohol was allowed, and neither were 'heathen' games; and no stranger was allowed to spend the night without permission from the mission authorities. Huts and livestock had to be kept in good condition. Failure to comply with these rules meant instant banishment, a life on the run as a *droster* or a pitiful existence as a farm labourer.

Every mission station seemed to specialise in one or two skills, depending on the expertise of the missionaries. Elim was well known for its thatchers and excellent butchery, Genadendal produced coveted knives and Wupperthal became famous for its shoes.

The factory was established in 1834 by a German shoemaker, Christian Häfele, who had come out to help Leipoldt in his work. Today it still operates but has been superseded by the highly efficient Strassberger Veldshoe Factory in Clanwilliam.

When Leipoldt died in 1872, he wasn't to know that his family name would become a household one in South Africa. His grandson was doctor and author C. Louis Leipoldt who is buried in one of his favourite spots at the top of the winding, beautiful Pakhuis Pass.

When you leave Wupperthal, you head up the Kouberg and can either stay on the main gravel road back to Clanwilliam or, if you have a vehicle that allows some exploring, take the very back roads that bump and grind you through the settlements of Wittewater and Heuningvlei.

Now you can take a donkey *karretjie* from the top of Pakhuis Pass down into Heuningvlei, spend a night with a local family and then head home the next day. It's a trip that will make you shake your head in wonder. Are you really only three hours from Cape Town where there are all-night bars, internet cafés and a million cars clogging the city's highways each day? This little village is made up of just over 20 families who work the vegetable gardens, keep a few sheep and grow rooibos tea.

Heuningvlei, according to Peter Slingsby and Ed Coombe in *Beyond the Cederberg – Agter-Pakhuis Biedouw Wupperthal*, has an interesting history. 'Once the property of the Ockhuis family, it was ceded to the Wupperthal mission as repayment for a debt. The Ockhuis family still live in the village ... in the old days the entire community would have moved to Sandwerf for the winter grazing. This once led to a tragedy, when a young cowherd shot himself after losing some cattle to a leopard. The path from Heuningvlei to Sandwerf is consequently reputed to be haunted, and is never used after dark!'

Previous spread *Step back in time and take a donkey cart ride from the top of Pakhuis Pass to the picturesque Heuningvlei where you can spend a night. Annie Ockhuis is just one of the residents who'll welcome you to Heuningvlei.*

This spread *In the small mission station of Wupperthal, shoemakers still put the skills they learnt from their forefathers to good use. During springtime, the N7 to Clanwilliam is a carpet of colour.*

Traveller's Rest

Haffie Strauss from Traveller's Rest has a reputation for making great *boerewors* and being a bit of a 'tough auntie'. The *boerewors* reputation is probably true. The tough auntie, well, maybe or maybe not. If you pop by you're likely to catch her busily doing the million things she does each day as she oversees the cottages and seasonal restaurant on the farm. Today she's in a hurry and off to see a new rock art painting that somebody has found on land they've just bought. It's a big elephant but a black cross has been scribbled over it. Fortunately, the cross is drawn in charcoal so will not be too difficult to remove.

The rock art on The Sevilla Trail at Traveller's Rest is spectacular, but you can be sure that what you get to see is a fraction of the treasures that have been painted in hidden-away caves and inaccessible places.

Back again at the homestead Haffie is taking a short break. Her house is crammed with books, paintings, papers, and objects found in the *veld*. There's an old *dassie karos* slung over the couch in the sunny lounge. It was made by her grandmother many years ago and is unbelievably warm – perfect for those icy mountain nights. Haffie comes from an old Cederberg family; her grandfather was Dr Nortier, one of C. Louis Leipoldt's best friends. She grew up in the area so the Cederberg landscape, with its strange rock formations and beautiful orange-hued mountains, is what she knows and loves best. But farming here is hard work. Farmers in the district used to grow potatoes, onions, melons and sweetcorn, but now transport over the Pakhuis Pass has become so expensive that it makes little or no economic sense planting cash crops that end up costing you money.

Haffie and Koos, her husband, are exploring other avenues. They're starting to plant various lavender, geranium and camomile varieties from which they plan to extract essential oils. They have also registered a species of granadilla plant that they have named Charité, after Haffie's mother and daughter. Dr Nortier, Haffie's grandfather, chose interesting names for his daughters. There's Charité, Clemencé, Joy and, finally, Amnesté, when he finally made peace with the idea of having four daughters and no son to carry on the family name!

The Strausses are also very interested in researching whether the indigenous plants that grow in the area can't be used for medicinal purposes. 'The San have been using plants from the *veld* for centuries,' explains Koos, 'and there's growing interest from academic institutions to see what role they can play in boosting the immune system against diseases such as cancer, TB and HIV/AIDS. I also know that the older people have a wealth of information that we are at risk of losing if we don't begin to record their indigenous knowledge. But it's a tricky business. The older people will talk to me, but some farmers treat them with disrespect, so they remain wary. It has taken years to build up a relationship with them. Each time I make a plan to sit down and have a serious talk to

strange rock formations and orange-hued mountains

one of these elderly people, I hear that they have died! They can show us things in the *veld* that we wouldn't notice no matter how many times we walked over it. This is the information that we stand to lose and we'll be the poorer for it.'

The Strausses aren't just interested in the *veld* for medicinal plants, however, as Haffie keeps an eagle eye out for a plant known as *veldkool, hottentotskool* or *bokkool*. 'You don't find a lot of them, but when you do they are absolutely delicious,' she says. 'There's a hint of *waterblommetjies* about them, but they taste even nicer, and if you cook them with lamb then you have a feast. But it must be good lamb to start with.'

Also on Haffie's menu of traditional *boerekos* delicacies, which she prepares at her small restaurant, Khoisan Kitchen, during August and September at the peak of the flower season, are curried offal, *kop en pootjies*, *roosterbrood* and best of all, Haffie's granadilla ice cream *(see right)*. The tart sweetness of the fruit, combined with the richness of cream is blissful. And, if you take a bowl outside while you admire the surreal Cederberg landscape with each fast-melting mouthful, it's about as close to heaven on earth as you're likely to get.

Meanwhile, back to the *boerewors*. 'Oh, I don't have any of it at the moment,' laughs Haffie.

'But come to think about it we have just bought a new bull so we will have to do something with the old one ...'

Haffie's granadilla ice cream

1 tin evaporated milk, cooled overnight
1 tin sweetened condensed milk
250ml cream
fresh pulp from about 30 granadillas (at least 3 cups)

Beat evaporated milk until double in volume. Add condensed milk and cream and beat lightly while slowly adding granadilla pulp until mixture suddenly thickens. Put in freezer for ice cream or use as thick cream to serve with fruit salad.

This spread *No country town is complete without a delicious array of home-made produce that you'll want to carry off with you. Women in Wupperthal produce melt-in-the-mouth chicken pie and biscuits, while Haffie Strauss from Traveller's Rest is famous for her* boerewors *and* kop en pootjies *(head and trotters), which she serves at her seasonal restaurant, Khoisan Kitchen.*

Clanwilliam and surrounds

The pretty town of Clanwilliam is the gateway to the Cederberg: modern-day travellers do just as the old-timers did and stock up on supplies before disappearing into the mountains. But, there's good reason to linger in the town. Each August, Clanwilliam comes alive with the spring flower show when every available venue is crammed with nature's bounty. The Clanwilliam Dam is also a firm favourite. The water skiing and fishing is top-notch and finding a house on the water's edge is a bonus. From here you can also easily explore the small towns further north, including Klawer, Vanrhynsdorp and Koekenaap – all brilliant during the flower season.

Dr C. Louis Leipoldt

The epitome of the Renaissance man, Dr Louis Leipoldt was well known as an Afrikaans poet, doctor, writer, botanist and chef. He grew up in the area, and there's a room devoted to him at the local museum. The simple grave under a rocky overhang on the Pakhuis Pass says a lot about the man who came from a long line of ministers and yet refused to have a pastor at his funeral.

Leipoldt never married, but his life was filled with friends and food. Author Lawrence Green in *Secrets of the Kombuis* describes Leipoldt's love of the food from the area. He writes, 'Leipoldt spoke of the little-known sea foods he enjoyed as a boy when the family trekked down to Lambert's Bay to escape the Clanwilliam heat. Mussel soup with milk and cream was one dish; mussel fritters was another, the shellfish blended with parsley, curry powder and wine. They ate the albatross in those days, known as *malmok*, that large and splendid ocean bird. It was hung for days, marinaded in wine vinegar, and braised with onions.

'Paw-paws were grown in many Clanwilliam gardens, for the heat suited sub-tropical fruits. People called the paw-paw "bobotie fruit" because this finely cut curried meat was often served with paw-paw leaves for flavouring. Leipoldt thought the paw-paw tasted at its best when mashed in a pudding with sugar and spices, ginger and eggs, and steamed in a cloth. They also made a paw-paw soup in Clanwilliam, using the green fruit, and they never failed to add the right amount of sherry.

'The *boerewors* of Clanwilliam, I gathered from Leipoldt, possessed qualities such as city butchers have never been able to achieve. Beef gave it bulk, though pork and mutton were added; and it was flavoured with such things as powdered ginger and mace, cloves and nutmeg, fennel and coriander, thyme and rosemary, sage, mint and garlic. Wine, vinegar and brandy were worked into this heroic formula and then the whole mixture was forced into the long skins. Leipoldt declared that *boerewors* should be grilled in the open on a fire of *renosterbos*; but in Clanwilliam the sausage was sometimes sun-dried like biltong.'

Today the local butchers still pride themselves on their excellent *wors*. Abrie Koekemoer from Clanwilliam Slaghuis believe the secret lies in the spices, which are much the same as they would have used in Leipoldt's time, and a healthy dose of vinegar and Worcester Sauce for extra flavour.

Strassbergers Veldshoe Factory

You could be forgiven for thinking that the names Grant, T.C., J.J., Daleen, Heinie, Romeo and Juliet were just like any other. Instead, they are the names of the lasts you'll see at the Strassbergers Veldshoe Factory in Clanwilliam, designating family members and top customers.

At 7:30, the factory is already humming and men in worn aprons work at lightning speed. *Velskoene*, or vellies, as they're fondly known, have been fundamental to this area since the early 1830s thanks to Johann Gotlieb Leipoldt, the German missionary responsible for the establishment of the mission station at Wupperthal. He believed that the manufacturing of shoes would not only provide job opportunities, but would help kick-start the industrial development of Wupperthal and the surrounding region.

The history of shoemaking in the area is bound up closely with Erna du Plessis' family. Her dad, Heinie, played a pivotal role in the establishment of the current shoe factory and its subsequent move to Clanwilliam.

'Shoemaking at Wupperthal went through many ups and downs over the decades,' explains Erna. 'In 1953 tough decisions had to be made. When Heinie Strassberger's five-year contract expired, the church wished to restore the businesses at Wupperthal to their former status under the mission's control. This would have left Heinie with an uncertain future, so he decided to uproot his family and start a shoe factory in Clanwilliam. The two hard-working Strassberger brothers, Heinie and Reinholdt, saw the Strassberger empire grow until they owned the hotel, the shoe factory, three farms, mills, a transport business, shops and a garage. 'When the factory moved to Clanwilliam, many of the coloured workers moved with Heinie and in this way the family tradition of involvement in the shoe industry continued. Slons Meyer, the last member who moved with us from Wupperthal, died on 16 July 2005. Then there's Niklaas Julies, who has been working at Strassbergers for 48 years. His two sons and daughter are still actively involved, as are three of his grandchildren.'

Today the factory turns out around 300 pairs of shoes per day, which are delivered around the country and to a few overseas clients who order regularly. If it's the personal touch you prefer then no import is going to do it for you. Erna explains what makes a good shoe: 'It is the quality of the leather, the comfort and good fit and excellent craftsmanship. And because we're a family-run business we get to know our customers and are able to give them customised service. We very often have to make special shoes for victims of polio, and other crippled feet. One of our customers has size 16 feet and we're able to make him really comfortable shoes.'

Two of their more unusual customers were the donkeys that drew a cart along Adderley Street. The colour of choice? Pink, of course!

Do the family wear their own shoes? 'Absolutely!' laughs Erna.

'The only downside which isn't good for the bottom line is that they are too comfortable and last far too long ...'

This spread *The Clanwilliam Dam is a riot of colour during spring and each year attracts hundreds of water enthusiasts.*

intermediary between the physical world and the spiritual world

Bushmans Kloof Wilderness Reserve and Retreat

There can't be that many luxury lodges in South Africa that have a good collection of Africana along with titles in Arabic and Chinese. But Bushmans Kloof is hardly run of the mill. The property has over 130 known San rock art sites, some dating back 10 000 years, and the Bushmans Kloof team is committed to doing everything they can to preserve this rich cultural treasure. Their efforts have been recognised in Bushmans Kloof being awarded South African Natural Heritage status.

Things weren't always so rosy for this farm on the top of the Cederberg. Before its transformation it was known as Boontjieskraal, and when the farm was sold in the 1980s, it was over-grazed and run down. Farming in this region is unbelievably difficult and the land carries the scars of years of failed attempts.

It will take decades for the *veld* to return to its natural state, but that hasn't dampened the team's enthusiasm. They all have a clear sense of working for a much bigger picture and are happy to pass up on instant gratification. Only game endemic to the area has been reintroduced, which includes wildebeest, Cape mountain zebra, eland, genet, mongoose, blesbok, brown hyena, and the endangered bontebok that was all but wiped out by our trigger-happy ancestors. Bushmans Kloof is also a proud sponsor of The Cape Leopard Trust and the game rangers are hoping to see more leopard spoor in the sandy soil.

But, while the flora and fauna are fascinating, it's the rock art at Bushmans Kloof that's really memorable. The man to help you make sense of it all is Siyakha Mguni, a rock art archaeologist, who was appointed into the position of resident archaeologist and curator at Bushmans Kloof in July 2005. There's some delicious irony in a young man of 33 unpacking the secrets of art that's tens of thousands of years old.

Siyakha divides his time between on-site research and working at the Clanwilliam-based Living Landscape Project. His main job at Bushmans Kloof is to record, document and research all of the 135 known sites, plus any potential new sites on the reserve, and to create a database linked to a Geographic Information System (GIS). This database will culminate in an integrated Rock Art Management Plan that can be used as a standard in the region for similar situations. He also works closely with the other Bushmans Kloof rangers to ensure that they're up to date with current research and interpretation of the art. Siyakha is passionate about the job at hand and in awe of the art he studies on a daily basis.

'For centuries, people believed that rock art was simply a record of what happened during the daily life of the San,' explains Siyakha. 'But post-1970, this began to shift, and there's an understanding that the art is much richer, and carries enormous spiritual meaning that tells us of the inner lives of the San. The art is riddled with metaphors and it's unpacking the rich symbolism that is such a challenge for us. Our understanding is evolving all the time and that's really exciting.'

Siyakha continues, 'Take images of the eland, for instance. This is the largest antelope in Africa and very rich in fat – just think of the dewlaps on an eland bull. For the /Xam people (a San clan), fat was incredibly significant both practically and spiritually because they thought that the eland was imbued with supernatural powers. The /Xam believed that the eland was created first and fed on honey, which explains why it grew so big and fat. And so it's from the eland that they draw an enormous amount of power. To this day, you only have to think about the San in the Kalahari when they hunt an eland. When the beast is killed, there's a lot of ritual that takes place to enable them to draw on the animal's potency. Drawings of an eland are not simply depictions of animals that they've seen or hope to hunt. Rather the eland serves as an intermediary between the physical world and the spiritual world.'

For Siyakha, rock art is more than just his career: 'Studying San art is not just an academic pursuit, it also affords insight into those great values of humanity from the past – values that, unfortunately, we seem to have shed – that held in balance our oldest societies for many millennia. These are as relevant and pragmatic today as they were in the past.'

This spread *Bushmans Kloof Wilderness Reserve and Retreat has some of the best San rock art you can hope to find in the Cederberg and each site is carefully mapped and recorded for posterity.*

Elands Bay and Verlorenvlei

Pull on your wetsuit, grab your surfboard and head for the sea. Elands Bay is every surfer's West Coast mecca, their Holy Grail or Nirvana, and is described as 'way cool' by youngsters and ageing sea rats alike.

It's a combination of things that make this little bay, which is about two-and-a-half hours' drive from Cape Town, so popular. A rocky shelf helps produce an awesome hollow wave that runs for more than 150m. E-bay, as it's fondly known among surfing aficionados, is also well loved for its perfect left-hand waves. There are days when the wind pumps along the West Coast, but during the holiday season this surf spot often becomes so busy that you will need to get up early if you want any of the waves for yourself.

A good place to park off when you're not in the briny blue is the Elands Bay camping ground situated right on the beach. Be warned – sturdy tent pegs might be needed to prevent your accommodation taking off and ending up 100km away.

If you tire of surfing (as if!) you can also spend a day paddling on Verlorenvlei, which flows into the Atlantic Ocean at Elands Bay. The vlei stretches for over 30km and this wetland has been identified as one of the country's important Bird Areas and is a Ramsar listed site. There's some concern, however, that the survival of the vlei is being threatened by farmers who pump water from the wetland to irrigate their thirsty cash crops.

You can hire boats for the day from Mike Barris, who lives opposite the hotel, for around R200 for a tandem canoe. All you'll need are strong arm muscles and plenty of refreshments to keep you going. The bird life on the vlei is rated as some of the best on the West Coast. You'll see plenty of pelicans, spoonbills and coots. A feather in any birder's cap is spotting the brightly coloured purple gallinule – unmistakable with its indigo plumage and bright red beak. As they are relatively common in the area, even if you don't see a bird, you're likely to hear them as they make a variety of harsh shrieks, wails and booming notes.

If it's a sense of history you're after, it's a short walk up to Elands Bay Cave where you can see rock art hand prints that bear testimony to the bay's first residents who lived here thousands of years ago.

Red gold – West Coast crayfish

It's not just the Cape fur seals, hagfish, mussel crackers and tuna that find the West Coast rock lobster (*Jasus lalandii*) prime pickings. There are few visitors to the West Coast who'll pass up on the opportunity of a delicious crayfish meal. If you can, diving for crayfish is the best way to ensure a fantastic feast. They taste best cooked on the coals, with plenty of lemon butter. Eat them in your swimming costume so it doesn't matter how messy you get! Permits can be obtained from your local post office and the main 'cray' season runs from mid-November to end of January.

If you don't feel like braving the icy West Coast waters for this delicacy, any number of the local restaurants have crayfish on the menu. Wendy Coetzee from the appropriately named Die Kreefhuis (The Crayfish House) suggests you try their speciality, Crayfish Romano. It's not dissimilar to a Crayfish Thermidor, but the secret lies in the cheese and garlic sauce. Delicious!

To protect the valuable red gold from over fishing, it's illegal to buy crayfish from street vendors. So remember to buy from a licensed dealer or quota holder.

This spread *Purple flowers create a magical carpet of colour at Bushmans Kloof Wilderness Reserve and Retreat.*

Following spread *Elands Bay is a well-known surfer's mecca where water rats spend hours in the icy waves and rave about Elands' perfect left-hand break. Afterwards they gather to share stories over a drink at the local hotel. Moonrise and sunset are captured at Elands Bay on the same day.*

Lambert's Bay

The sleepy town of Lambert's Bay is pretty quiet for most of the year, but come summer hols the town is packed with holidaymakers who love the area's isolation and laid-back friendliness. People heading up the West Coast aren't interested in putting on the glitz – they're happiest in their shorts and T-shirts and come for the wide spaces, spectacular wind-swept beaches and great fishing.

Head for Bird Island when you're there. It's just off the harbour and the causeway makes for easy access. This is a sensory experience! Not only is the smell of guano pretty potent depending on which way the wind is blowing, but the thousands of birds that breed here announce their arrival and departure, so the air rings with gannet and gull 'talk'. Bird Island is one of only six sites in the world where the Cape gannet breeds and you can watch them from comfortable hides that give you a bird's-eye view. Observe how the birds circle a few times before landing on the 'runway' at the perimeter of the hurly burly. Once they hit the ground, they wrestle their way to their nests through a seething mass of noisy counterparts, who peck and harass them as they go!

A report issued in November 2005 suggests that life on Bird Island might not be that secure for the gulls and gannets. The threat comes from the booming Cape fur seal population, which was introduced to the area in 1985. Research by CapeNature estimates that since the latter 1990s, 8 000 birds have been killed by the seals so making a serious dent in the 11 000 breeding pairs that are usually recorded here between August and March. Solutions are being sought, but just what to do to save this threatened bird population remains a conundrum.

Plaaskombuis

After an early morning out on the beach, a great way to spend the rest of the day is at one of the open-air seafood restaurants in the area. Alternatively, you can head inland and have a leisurely lunch at Kitta Burger's Plaaskombuis on her farm Steenbokfontein, where she serves up delicious West Coast meals using recipes passed on from her mom and grandmother. It's appropriate considering her restaurant is in what used to be the original house built in 1864. This is slow food at its best. Everything is cooked on a blackened Dover stove in big old pots. What comes out of them is delicious – smoked mussel soup *(see right)*, anise sweet potato, lamb stew that is so tender it falls off the bone, green bean *bredie*, home-made bread, Kitta's preserves, *koeksisters* and coffee.

But, apart from making wonderful *boerekos*, Kitta is also the keeper of family history. It all started around 1830 with two orphans who were adopted by Gerrit Erasmus Smit, the then owner of Steenbokfontein. When he passed away, one Burger youngster inherited Steenbokfontein, while the other inherited Karringmelkvlei near Citrusdal.

The family's history is intricately bound up with the wreck of the HMS *Sybille*, which ran aground in 1901 on the rocks of the seaside border of the farm. Rescue operations began immediately and an engineer, Harry Blades, was sent from England to help with the salvage. Martjie (Martha) Burger, the young daughter of farmer Burger was 15 when she met Harry Blades and fell instantly in love with the handsome young engineer. But her family would hear none of it and it was only when she came of age on her 21st birthday that she was allowed to marry him. They were married twice – first at the church in Leipoldtville in Afrikaans and then at the Groote Kerk in Cape Town in English. Soon after, they left for England, never to return.

'But,' continues Kitta, 'her children have been back to the farm on a number of occasions and in 2005 we had a family reunion. It was lovely to meet that branch of the family and they have very fond memories of the farm – obviously from what Martha had told them about growing up on the West Coast.'

Steenbokfontein's recent history is captivating, but it's also exceptionally rich in even earlier history. Excavations have uncovered objects that date back at least 8 500 years; there are rock paintings in caves on the farm and recently old stone kraals from 700 years ago were uncovered. It is also home to a unique black lizard that only occurs in the area.

Kitta's famous creamy mussel soup

1 onion, finely chopped
1 clove garlic, crushed
30g butter
60ml dry white wine
12,5ml chopped parsley
salt and freshly ground black pepper to taste
25ml flour
500ml long life homogenised milk
125ml cream
1 chicken stock block dissolved in 200ml warm water
12,5ml lemon juice
400g mussel meat or tinned mussels drained of all excess oil

Sauté onion and garlic in butter. Add wine. Mix together the dry ingredients. Add the milk, cream, chicken stock and lemon juice to this mixture and add to the onion and garlic. Bring to the boil. Add the mussel meat and heat through. Serve warm with chopped parsley on top and warm home-made bread. This serves 3–4 people.

This spread *Hike to the top of Bobbejaan's Point overlooking Elands Bay and you'll find miniature Zen gardens artfully captured among the rocks. Elands Bay at sunset.*

Following spread *There are plenty of open-air seafood restaurants all the way up the West Coast where you can enjoy some of the freshest fish, crayfish and mussels. This archival photo, circa 1925, was taken at Lambert's Bay and shows West Coast crayfish, also known as red gold, being hauled from the sea. A packet of* slap chips *– perfect surfer's chow.*

Favourites

You can't leave the area without:

- **Taking a leap of faith and booking a tandem skydiving experience** in Citrusdal. The scenery from the air is breathtaking and you have an excellent view over the entire valley.
- **Lolling in the warm mineral pools** at one of the hot springs in Citrusdal. Taking the waters has been considered restorative for centuries.
- **Striking out on one of the many hikes in the Cederberg.** You'll be hard pressed to choose – the legendary Wolfberg Cracks, the Maltese Cross, or Malgat to swim in the pools? Whatever your choice, go prepared. For longer and more strenuous routes, wear the correct hiking clothes and take plenty of water, some food and an emergency thermal blanket. If you can, let somebody know where you are hiking and when you plan (roughly) to be back.
- **Finding some rock art to marvel at.** The route at Traveller's Rest is easy to follow and well signposted – great if you only have a morning to do some exploring. If you prefer a guided tour of rock art sites, the Clanwilliam Living Landscape Project has knowledgeable guides who offer a fascinating trip to Warmhoek, a trail 10 minutes out of Clanwilliam that is rich in rock art.
- **Splashing out on a stay at the fabulous Bushmans Kloof Wilderness Reserve and Retreat.** The accommodation is world-class, the food outstanding and there's a luxurious spa where you can experience some serious pampering after going on a nature drive or a rock art expedition with expertly trained guides.
- **Stocking up on a stash of wine** from Cederberg Cellars at Dwarsrivier. Try the Chenin Blanc, which wins one award after the other, as does the Shiraz. The Sauvignon Blanc keeps getting better and sells out quickly. Keep an eye out for news of their new sparkling wine.
- **Eating warm bread** that's been baked in a roadside clay oven. Try it with lots of butter and some home-made preserves.
- **Visiting the Clanwilliam Ramskop Wildflower Garden** in August. This is also when the Clanwilliam Flower Show takes place in the old Dutch Reformed church and almost every available space in town is filled with flowers. The erstwhile Clanwilliam gaol is now a museum and also well-worth visiting.
- **Buying a pair of *velskoene*** from the factory at Wupperthal or at Strassbergers Veldshoe Factory in Clanwilliam. Make sure you like them, as they're going to last a long time.
- **Finding a good camp site** (Sanddrif is an excellent choice) and settling in for a few days really to unwind. Take books, hiking boots, some great wine and a pack of cards. Good company is also essential. Don't forget a head torch!
- **Stocking up on home produce** on one of the many farm stalls you'll pass. There are oranges in season, dates, bags of rooibos tea and enough jams and preserves to fill a groaning ox wagon. Keep a look out for some locally made liqueurs as well. Craig Royston stocks a granadilla liqueur that is delicious and smells of hot February days.
- **Visiting Bird Island** at Lambert's Bay. It's one of only six sites in the world where Cape gannets breed and it's amazing to watch this seething mass of birds. The whiff of guano is pretty potent, depending on which way the wind is blowing.
- **Tucking into some home-made chicken pie** at Wupperthal.
- **Taking a trip back in time** and travelling by donkey cart from the top of Pakhuis Pass to the small village of Heuningvlei, where you can spend a night with a local family.
- **Having a meal at the Plaaskombuis** on Steenboksfontein farm just outside Lambert's Bay. Kitta Burger cooks everything the old-fashioned way on a wood-fired stove and wouldn't dream of serving anything but excellent West Coast fare. There's anise sweet potato, green bean *bredie*, lamb stew and home-made bread. Don't forget to book ahead.
- **Tackling a local 4x4 route.** There are plenty to choose from but the road from Matjiesrivier to Wupperthal is a good start. It'll take you around two hours; you don't really need a 4x4 but high clearance is essential. The views and *fynbos* along the way are spectacular and the sense of isolation awe-inspiring.

Tourism Bureaux

Citrusdal Tourism: (022) 921-3210

Clanwilliam Tourism: (027) 482-2024

Graafwater Tourism: (027) 422-1108

Lambert's Bay Tourism: (027) 432-1000

Leipoldtville Tourism: (027) 432-1000 or (027) 412-2116

Contact Numbers

Bird Island: 082 455 5992

CapeNature: www.capenature.org.za

Cederberg donkey cart trip: (022) 931-2900

Cederberg Wines: (027) 482-2827, www.cederbergwine.com

Clanwilliam Living Landscape Project: (027) 482-1911, www.cllp.uct.ac.za/

Craig Royston: (022) 921-2963

Die Kreefhuise: (027) 432-2235

Old Gaol Museum: (027) 482-2024

Ramskop Wildflower Garden: (027) 482-8000

Skydive Citrusdal: (021) 462-5666 or 083 462 5666, www.skydive.co.za

Strassbergers Veldshoe Factory: (027) 482-2141

Where to stay

The Baths, Citrusdal: (022) 921-8026/7, www.thebaths.co.za

Bushmanskloof: (027) 482-2627, www.bushmanskloof.co.za

Elands Bay Campsite and Caravan Park: 072 603 3141

Lambert's Bay Hotel: (027) 432-1126

Leipoldt's Country Retreat: (027) 412-2116

Sandrift on Dwarsrivier farm: (027) 482-2827

Strassberger's Hotel Clanwilliam: (027) 482-1101, www.clanwilliam.info/hotel

Traveller's Rest: (027) 482-1824, www.travellersrest.co.za

This spread *The West Coast – from Yzerfontein to Elands Bay, through to Lambert's Bay and then beyond to Doringbaai – puts on a great show each sunset.*

Glossary

Allesverloren	All is lost
baie	very
bakkie	pick-up truck
balseminie	balsam plant
berg	mountain
bietjie	little, bit
blanke	white person
blaar/blare	leaf/leaves
blerrie	bloody (slang)
bliksem	damn
blom	flower
bobotie	curried mince dish
boer(e)	farmer(s)
boerekos	country food
boereseun	farm boy
bokbaaivygie	*Mesembryanthemum* spp.
bokkom	dried Cape herring or mullet
boksuring	*Oxalis* spp.
bontebok	pied antelope
bossiesveld	bush shrub
braai	barbecue
bredie	stew of meat and vegetables
dak	roof
dakkamer	loft room
dassie	rock rabbit
die	the
dogter	daughter
dominee	minister of religion
donder	hit
donga	gully
dorpie	small town
drif	ford
droëwors	dried sausage
droster	deserter
duiker	small antelope
duiker, witbors-	whitebreasted cormorant
eerbaarheid	integrity
eers(te)	first
Engels	English
erf/erven	plot/s of land
fontein	spring
fris	healthy/well-built
fynbos	scrubby vegetation endemic to the Western Cape
gaan maar aan	just carry on
galjoen	blackfish
gasvryheid	hospitality
gees	spirit
gemaklik(e)	comfortable
gemeng(de)	mixed
gemsbok	oryx
gogga	insect
gooi	throw
harder	Cape herring, mullet
hartebees	type of antelope
huiskind	homebody
jag	chase
jong/jonk	young
karos	animal skin rug or throw
karretjie	animal-drawn cart
karwyder	transporter
kleindogter	granddaughter
klomp	bunch, crowd
kloof	gorge
koeksister	a plaited, fried, syrupy sweet
kombuis	kitchen
kop	head
kos	food
kuier	visit
lek	leak
lui	lazy
lus	desire
maak die hek toe ass(eblief)	please close the gate
mal	mad
melktert	milk tart
misvloer	packed dung floor
moeilik	difficult
mootjie	fillet of fish
Môredou	Morning dew
Môreson	Morning sun
Môrester	Morning star
'n	a/an
nagmaal	holy communion
nie blanke	non-white person
nuut/nuwe	new
ongegun(d)	begrudged
oom/omie	uncle (familiar)
opskop	dance/informal party
ouma	grandmother
oupa	grandfather
pad	road
pakhuis	warehouse
predikant	minister of religion
reg(te)	right, real
riempie	thin strip of leather
rooikat	caracal
roosterbrood	toast
rustigheid	peacefulness
Sandveld	sandy countryside
selfstandig(e)	independent/ self-reliant
seun	boy
siekte	illness
skiet	shoot
skinder	gossip
skottel	dish-like barbecue
slap	limp/floppy (used for chips as opposed to crisps)
smoor	braise
smous	hawker
smulgoed	snacks
snoek	sea pike
snoekkuit(e)	sea pike roe
spanspek	sweet melon
spens	pantry
steenbras	steenbras (fish)
stoep	verandah
strandloper	literally 'beach walker' – member of the Khoikhoi tribe (now extinct) who lived off sea food
suring	sorrel
tannie	aunt (familiar)
treknet	drag net
tuisgebak(te)	home-baked
uitlander	foreigner
veld	field, countryside
vel(d)skoen (vellie)	soft leather shoe
vlakte	plain
vlei	marsh
vygie	mesem
waterblommetjie	Cape pondweed
Weskusser	inhabitant of the West Coast
wildebeest	gnu
witblits	a raw, white spirit
wynland	wine-growing area

This spread *Groot Paternoster Reserve.*

West Coast Annual Events

See pages listed for contact numbers and addresses to obtain specific dates for events.

Town	Events	When to visit
Aurora *(See pg 147)*	• Endurance Ride (March) • Dance (July) • Aurora Show (Aug)	Enjoy hiking in winter and spectacular flowers in spring. The clear winter skies are also excellent for stargazing.
Citrusdal *(See pg 199)*	• 2x4x4 Weekend (Apr) • Olifants River Canoe Race (Aug) • Citrus Festival (Aug)	The Cederberg mountain range is right on your doorstep and you can use Citrusdal as a base for hiking, visiting rock art sites and relaxing in the local hot springs. The landscape bursts into colour during spring when the flowers are out.
Clanwilliam *(See pg 199)*	• Agricultural Show (Apr) • Eleven o'clock Rooibos Festival (Apr) • Cederberg Endurance Walk (May) • Flower Show (Aug) • Food & Wine Festival (Sept) • Wild Flower Show (Sept) • Bass Classic Fishing Tournament (Oct) • Rooibos Triathlon and Fitness Festival (Oct)	Every season has its own charm. Autumn offers clear, warm days ideal for exploring the region and perfect for trying out one of the many hikes in the area. It's cold in winter but you may be lucky enough to experience snow on the mountain peaks. In spring, the landscape is transformed into a blazing carpet of colour and the annual flower show will see the town packed to capacity. It's hot here in summer so be sure to find a crystal clear rock pool to wallow in.
Darling *(See pg 51)*	• Saturday Morning Market (Monthly) • Passion Play (Easter) • Winter Solstice Ball (June) • Evita se Perron: Voorkamer Festival (Sept) • Duckitt Nursery's Orchid Show (Sept) • Darling Wild Flower Show (Sept) • Evita se Perron: Christmas Season (Dec)	Darling is the perfect getaway throughout the year. Spring is wildflower season and also when the Darling Wildflower Show, Duckitt Nurseries Orchid Show and the Voorkamerfest take place. Winter is the green season – relax in front of a roaring log fire with a glass of one of the excellent local wines in a guesthouse. Visit the remarkable museums or an art gallery. Summer is the busy harvest time; and pristine beaches are only 15 minutes away at the coastal town of Yzerfontein. Throughout the year enjoy cabaret, drama and comedy at Evita se Perron theatre; play a game of golf or bowls; or visit a nature reserve.
Goedverwacht *(See pg 147)*	• Snoek and Soet Patat Festival (July) • Heritage Weekend (Sept)	There's something magical about this little village throughout the year and you'll experience warm hospitality regardless of the weather. In spring, the mountainside and verges are covered with flowers and the mountain fynbos and protea put on a brilliant show. Don't miss taking the back route from the village to the top of the Piketberg mountain range during spring.
Lambert's Bay *(See pg 199)*	• Crayfish Festival (March) • Steenbokfontein Art Celebration (Sept) • Beer Festival (Oct) • Golf Classic (Nov) • Miss Lambert's Bay/ Rooidop Opskop (Dec)	The gannets and cormorants that throng Bird Island will thrill bird lovers throughout the year. Lambert's Bay also has some wonderfully isolated beaches that are superb during summer when the water is (slightly) less bracing than usual. You'll be able to find an isolated spot far from any crowds. Any day during the season is a good time to visit one of the open-air seafood restaurants in the area for a real taste of West Coast hospitality.

Town	Events	Description
Langebaan *(See pg 99)*	• Arts & Crafts Market (Monthly) • Club Mykonos: Offshore Surfski, Sailing regatta, WP Triathlon, Lazor Nationals (Feb) • Road/Air Show (Apr) • Stompneus Derby (Apr) • Club Mykonos: Cycle Tour (May) • Club Mykonos: NSRI Food & Wine Festival (Sept) • Black Mussel Festival (Oct) • Yacht Club Potjiekos Competition (Nov) • Club Mykonos: NSRI Miss Bikini and Mnr Mykonos Lyf Competition (Dec)	This is an excellent year-round holiday destination with plenty to do. In the summer months when the wind is up, there is a diversity of lagoon water sports to enjoy – sailing, kite- and wind-surfing are among the most popular. Bird watching on the Langebaan Lagoon in the West Coast National Park is always rewarding and in spring a visit to Postberg to see the flowers is an absolute treat. During cooler months cycling through the park is one of the best ways to enjoy this unspoilt area. Don't forget to look out for whales towards the end of winter and early spring.
Paternoster *(See pg 99)*		Paternoster offers the ideal place to escape, and your best bet is to find a seaside cottage and disappear for a few days. Spring brings the whales and a wonderful flower display at the nearby Cape Columbine Nature Reserve.
Piketberg *(See pg 147)*	• Museum Day (May) • Dance (Aug) • Agricultural Show (Aug)	Head to the top of the Piketberg mountain in spring to admire the fruit blossoms that cover the farms in a delicate pink and white. The local flower show in August is also well worth a visit.
Porterville *(See pg 147)*	• Tour D'ville (Jan) • Gatskop Interclub Paragliding Competition (March) • Golf Club Annual Masters Competition (March) • Agricultural and Flower Show (Sept) • All Africa Paragliding Open Championship (Dec) • Serial Class Paragliding Competition (Dec)	It gets really hot in Porterville during summer, but this never deters the hang- and paragliders who flock to this sleepy agricultural town to experience some of the best flying in South Africa. Luckily there are plenty of mountain retreats and cool rock pools for you to laze in. In spring, the countryside is a verdant green punctuated by the brilliant yellow patches of the canola fields. Hiking is best done in the cooler months.
Riebeek Valley *(See pg 51)*	• Morning Market (Monthly) • Quilters Festival – every two years (May) • PPC – Berg River Marathon (Aug) • Riebeek-Kasteel Half-Marathon (Sept) • NG Church Festival (Sept) • Riebeek Valley Olive Festival (June)	Autumn transforms this picturesque valley into an artist's landscape when the vines turn a fantastic red and orange. This is also a great time to do some serious red wine tasting and stock up on good quality local port for the winter months. The Olive Festival in winter is also a highlight of the area and not to be missed.
Velddrif *(See pg 99)*	• Annual Berg River Dinghy Race (Dec) • Port Owen River Race (Jan) • Passion Play (March) • Berg River Canoe Marathon (July) • Alabama Festival (Aug)	Get out your fishing tackle – you've got both the sea and the river to enjoy during the summer months. This area is also a bird-watcher's paradise and the best viewing is normally from September to December. Look out for whales from August through to January, and the flowers are usually magnificent from the end of July till the end of September depending on the rain.
Wupperthal *(See Clan-william p199)*	• Cederberg Voorbrand Festival (Apr) • Cultural Heritage Festival (Sept) • Carols by Candlelight (Dec)	Wupperthal is hot in summer and cold in winter. The best time to visit, depending on the rainfall, is August to October and March through to May. Go hiking in the mountains or explore one of the many enticing 4x4 routes in the area.
Yzerfontein *(See pg 51)*	• Bokbaai Vygie Route (Sept) • Snoek and Crayfish Derby & Beer Festival (Dec) • NG Church Bazaar (Dec) • Morning Market (Every last Saturday of the month)	Relaxing near the sea is good any time of the year, but if you want to see great flowers visit the area between August and October. If it's whales you are after August to April are the best months but they can be seen almost the whole year round. The winter waves are a must for serious photographers.

Index

Note: Page numbers in *italics* refer to photographs and maps.

4x4 route 198

A

Abrahamskraal *65*
African bear (*Agriotherium africanum*) 61
Algeria 169
Allesverloren
- farm 17, 27
- Port wine 50
- wine sales (contact number) 51

Anatolian Shepherds 171
Anglo-Boer War 152–153
- memorabilia 150

annual events 202–203
Anreith, Anton 126
antelope 150, 189
Aurora 110–111
- annual events 202
- Tourism (contact number) 147
- Women's Network 110

B

balseminie plant (*Nemesia strumosa*) 40
Bartholomeus Klip Farmhouse 30–31, 50
- contact number 51

Baths, The 150, 152, 157
- contact number 199

beach
- houses *56*
- vegetation 91, 92

Beach Camp, The 98
- contact number 99

Beaverlac holiday resort 134, 146
- contact number 147

beetle-smuggling ring 138
Bergius, Petrus Jonas (botanist) 136
Berg River 17, 86, *87*, 93, 95, 96, 98
- Boat Trips (contact number) 99
- Canoe Marathon 98
- Estuary *93*
- salt pans *94*

BHP Billiton mining company 61
Biedouw Valley 169
Bird Area 191
Bird Island 93, 195, 198
- contact number 199

birds 61, 191, 195
- hide 98
- West Coast Bird Club 93, 95

bird watching 98
blesbok 189
blue whale 63
boats for hire 191
Bobbejaan's Point *194*
boerewors 184, 187
Boer rebellion 18
bokbaaivygies 47
bokkom, *see* harder fish
bontebok 68, 189
Bryde's whale 63
buchu *124*, 124–125
- *Agathosma betulina* 124
- *Agathosma crenulata* 124

Buck Bay historic homestead 35
Bushman's Kloof
- contact number 199
- Wilderness Reserve 189, *190*, 198

C

Cabernet Sauvignon 162
camomile 184
canola fields 146
'Cape Breadbasket' *12*
Cape Columbine Nature Reserve 78, 98
Cape Floral Kingdom 91
Cape gannet 68
Cape Hangklip 17
Cape Leopard Trust 171, 189
CapeNature 138, 157, 195
- campsites 169
- contact number 199

CapeNature Conservation 138
- Environment Crime Investigation Unit (ECIS) 138

Cape Reeds (Restios) 91
Cape Sport Centre (contact number) 99
Carinus Bridge 93
cedar trees 157, *168*, 169
Cederberg 10, *156*, 157
- Cellars 162, *163*
- donkey cart trip (contact number) 199
- mountain range 150
- Observatory 166–167, 169
- Wilderness Reserve 169
- Wines (contact number) 199

church, Goedverwacht *103*
Churchhaven *55*, 72, 75, 98
- graveyard *73*

Churchill, Winston 18
Citrusdal 150, 152–153, 198
- annual events 202
- location map *150*
- Tourism (contact numbers) 199

citrus farms 150
Clanwilliam 183, 187, 198
- annual events 202
- cedar tree (*Widdringtonia cedarbergensis*) 167
- Dam *186*, 187
- Flower Show 198
- Living Landscape Project (contact number) 189, 198, 199
- Ramskop Wildflower Garden 198
- red fin minnow 157
- Tourism (contact numbers) 199
- yellow fish 157

Cloeteskraal farm 90
Cloof (contact number) 51
Cochoqua tribe 14
colophon beetle 138
coots 191
cormorant
- Cape 93, 95
- whitebreasted 93, 95

Craig Royston's farm stall 150
- contact number 199

crane, blue 138
crayfish 127, 191
Cruythoff, Pieter 14
cycling 146

D

Da Gama, Vasco 86
daisies *119*
daisy family (Asteraceae) 124
Darling 44, 47
- annual events 202
- Cellars (contact number) 51
- Tourism Bureau 51

Wildflower Show 50, 51
Wine Experience 50
Dasklip 137
Pass 134, *136–137*, 146
Dassen Island 93
de la Caille, Abbé 111
De Saldanha, Admiral Antonio 75
Disa uniflora (Lady in Red) 136, 146
Doc's Cave 75
dolphin
Benguela, *see* Heaviside's
fossils 61
Heaviside's (*Cephalorhynchus heavisidii*) 93
South African, *see* Heaviside's
Dolphin B&B (contact number) 99
Donkergat 62, 63
donkeys 176
carts *180*, 183
Doornkloof farm 14
dormouse, spectacled 157
drum majorettes *16*
Duckitt, Hildagonda 40, 47, 133
Duckitt Nurseries Orchid Show 50
contact number 51
Duckitt, William 44, 47
Dutch East India Company 17, 40, 68, 75, 126, 152
Dutch Reformed Church 126, 198
Dwarsrivier farm 169, 198

E

eland 189
Elands Bay 191, *192–193*
Campsite and Caravan Park (contact number) 199
Cave 191
Elandsberg Nature Reserve 30, 31
elephant 150
elf (shad) fish 59, 89
Elim mission station 105, 183
Elsenberg (historic farm) 127
Eselbank 176
Evita se Perron *46*, *49*, 50, 51
contact number 51
Excelsior farm 114, 146
contact number 147
Extra Virgin Olive Oil 22

F

Farmhouse Hotel, The (contact number) 99
farms, historic 14, 17, 35
farmstalls 198
feather trade 114
feral pigs 130
fired red minnow 157
fishing
expedition 98
quotas 81
flamingo
greater 68
lesser 68, 93
pink 98
flora and fauna 189
see also flowers
Floral Cottage (contact number) 51
Flower of the Gods, *see Disa uniflora*
flowers 68, 124
fynbos 31, *139*, 146
indigenous 91, 92, 184
wild 78, 115, *149*, 150
fossils 10, 61
Fourie, Jopie 18
fox
bat-eared 68
Cape 68
Friday Island (contact number) 99
fruit 150
fungus (*Phytophthora*) 122
fynbos 31, *139*, 146

G

galjoen fish 89
gallinule, purple 191
game 189
lodge 30
gannet, Cape 195, 198
Ganzekraal 35
gazania (*botterblom*) (*Gazania krebsiana*) 85
geelbek fish 68
Geelbek historic homestead 114
gemsbok 68
Genadendal mission station 105, 183
genet 189
Geographic Information System (GIS) 189
geraniums 184
gerbils 90
Gethyllis species 43
giraffid *Sivatherium hendeyi* (fossil) 61
Goedverwacht 102, 105, 146
annual events 202
church *107*
guest house (contact number) 147
hiking trails (contact numbers) 147
homestay (contact number) 147
location map *102*
Tourism (contact number) 147
goeveneursboontjies, see herebone
Gold of Africa Museum 126
gomphotheres (fossil) 61
Gousblom B&B (contact number) 147
Graafwater 10
Tourism (contact number) 199
granadilla plants 184
Groote Post 40, 47
cellar and restaurant (contact number) 51
homestead 35
picnic 50
wine farm *41*
Grootfontein Farm 134, 146
Groot Paternoster Nature Reserve *82, 97*
Grootrivier 169
Groot Winterhoek
Mountains 146
Nature Reserve 134, 147
Grotto Bay *33*
grunter fish 89

H

hang-gliding 137, 146
contact numbers 147
harder (*bokkom*) fish *71, 88*, 89, 98
harrier, black 93
hartebees, red 68
Hawthornia dwarf aloes 138
Hendrik Frieslaar (contact number) 147
herebone (beans) 146
Hermon 30
Heuningvlei 167, 183, 198
Hex River Mountains 136
hiking 134, 146, 169, 198
Hoedjiesbaai 72
Hoekie Guest House (contact number) 99
homesteads, historic 35

honey bell bush (*Freylinia visseri*) 92
Hopefield 126–127
  church 127, 146
  Tourism (contact number) 147
horse riding 146
houseboat 98
hyena, brown 189

I

Important Bird Areas (IBAs) 93, 95
indigenous plants
  kukumakranka 43
  renosterbos 14
  renosterveld 31
  see also fynbos, wildflowers
iris flowers 124
IUCN Red List 93
Iziko South African Museum (Cape Town) 61, 62

J

Jacob's Bay 35
Jakkalsfontein 36
Jewish settlers 114

K

Kalkoenkop farm 141
kalkoentjie flower
Kapokberg 40
Kasteelberg (Castle Mountain) 14, 122
Kasteelberg Country Inn & Bistro (contact number) 51
kayaking 98
Keegan, Frances 35
kelp (*Ecklonia maxima*) 39
Kersefontein 126–127, *127*, 146
  contact number 147
Khoekhoen clans 183
  fish traps and shell middens 86
Khoi 14, 157
  words 43
Khoikhoi 75
King Protea (*Protea cynaroides*) 122
kite-surfing 98
Klawer 187
  Vallei (Clover Valley) 40, 44, 47
  Vlei 41
Klein Drakenstein mountains 14
klipfish 35
Klipfontein farm 111
Kliphuis campsite 169
Klok se Poort 146
Kloovenburg Estate 22
  contact number 51
Koekeman-Sonqua people 14, 27
Koekenaap 187
Koringberg 122
  Tourism (contact number) 147
Kouberg 183
Kraalbaai 75, 98
Krakadouw 167
Kukumakranka 43
Kuttel, Mary Melck 35

L

Laaiplek 93
Lady Di protea 122
Lager Bay 35
Lambert's Bay 10, 198
  annual events 202
  Hotel 199
  Tourism (contact number) 199
Langebaan 10, 54, 59, 72
  annual events 203
  House Boats (contact number) 99
  Lagoon *52*, 59, 61, *69*
  location map *54*
  Tourism (contact number) 99
  Yacht Club *56*
Langebaanweg – A Record of Past Life 61
Langkloof 173
Langrietvlei (contact number) 147
lavender 184
  bushes *51*
League of Nations Agreement 63
Leipoldt, C. Louis 183, 187
Leipoldt's Country Retreat (contact number) 199
Leipoldtville Tourism (contact number) 199
leopard 157, 171
  spoor *170*
lions 150
lizard, armadillo 157
Lower Berg River Wetlands 93, 95

M

Malan, Daniël François 18
Malgas Island 68
Malgat 198
Malmesbury 14, 72
  bry (pronunciation) 22
Maltese Cross 157, 169, 198
Mammal Research Institute 62, 63
Mamre 50
  mission station 105, 183
Mandela, Nelson 48
map of West Coast *7*
Marine and Coastal Management 84, 89
Martin Melck House 126
Matjiesrivier 173, 198
  Cedar Nursery 167, 169
  Nature Reserve 169
McGregor, Helena 152
McGregor, James 152, 153, 157
Meerhof farm 14
Meerhof, Pieter 14
Melck, Julian *126*, 126, 127
Melck, Martin 126–127
message in a bottle 36, *37*
Mgonnemoa (head of Cochoqua) 14
mineral pools 198
mission stations 105
Modderfontein farm 14, 153
mongoose 189
Moordenaarsgat (Murderer's cave) 173
Moorreesburg Tourism (contact number) 147
mootjies (fillets) 35
Moravian Church 105
Moravian Mission 102
  Station 173
Moravians 106
Môrester farm 28
morning market 50
mountain biking 169
mountain climbing 169
Mountain Pride butterfly (*Meneris tulbaghia*) 136
Mount Ceder *154*,169
Mouton, Maria 30–31
museums
  Iziko South African Museum (Cape Town) 61, 62
mussels 36
  cured 98

N

Natural Heritage Site 146

O

octopus, pickled ('tjoka') *80*
Oesterwal historic homestead 35
Old Gaol Museum 199
Olifantsriver Mountains 134, 146
Olifants River
  Estuary 93
Oliphants River 150
Olive Boutique 24, 50
  contact number 51
olives *23, 25*
  curing of 24

extra virgin olive oil 22, 50
tasting 50
Ongegund farm 18
orchids 124, 136
Ormonde (contact number) 51
Oudrif 169
Overberg 17
Owen, Frederick John 134
owl, barn (*Tyto alba*) 90, 91
Oystercatcher's Haven (contact number) 99

P

Pakhuis Pass 169, 183, 198
paper flowers *164*
Paradise Farm 44
paragliding 137, 146
contact numbers 147
Parker, Dale 30
Paternoster 78, 81
annual events 203
Die Winkel op *78*
se Padstal 98, 99
Tourism (contact number) 99
pea flowers 124
Peerboom walk 146
Pelican Harbour Charters (contact number) 99
pelicans 98, 191
Pentz, Peter 40
Piekenaarskloof Pass *148*, 150
Piketberg 10, 102, 114
annual events 203
flower show 146
mountains *115*
Tourism (contact number) 147
Piket-Bo-Berg 105, 114
Piket-bo-berg Tea Garden 118, 146
contact numbers 147
Pilgrim's Rest historic farm 82
Plankiesbaai 68
poaching of game 138
porcupines 133
Port (wine) 27, 50
Porterville 134, 136
annual events 203
Cellars 146
farm dam *134*
Flyer's Lodge 137
Tourism (contact number) 147
Porter, William 134
Postberg 65
Nature Reserve 68
potjiekos challenge *116*
pottery *132*, 133
Pride of Table Mountain, *see Disa uniflora*
proteas 122, *123*, 146
purple laver (*Porphyra capensis*) 39

R

Ramsar (Wetlands Convention) Site 68, 95, 191
Ramskop Wildflower Garden (contact number) 199
Red Data Book 92
Red Disa (*Disa uniflora*) 136
recipes
Ansie's apricot biscuits 178
Ansie Vlok's quince jelly 28, *29*
Aunt Allie's porcupine preparation 133
Bokkoms 89
Haffie's granadilla ice cream 185
Home-made ginger beer 118
Isobel's *waterblommetjiebredie* 141
Kelp pickle 85
Kersefontein leg of wild boar 130
Kitta's famous creamy mussel soup 195
Nori (Porphyra) fritters 39
Pumpkin fritters 106
Stuffed harders or mullet 70
Sweet potato cake 118
West Coast caviar 70
Rhenish Missionary Society 183
renosterbos (*Elytropappus rhinocerotis*) 14, 91, 124, 187
renosterveld 31, 40, 91, 124
restaurants, coffee shops
Die Kreefhuis (The Crayfish House) 191, 199
Geelbek Restaurant 68, 98, 99
Hilda's Kitchen 40
Khoisan Kitchen 169, 185
L'Attitude Restaurant 17
Piketberg-bo-berg Tea Garden 119
Plaaskombuis 195, 198
Voorstrand Restaurant 84
Restios, *see* Cape Reeds
Riebeek-Kasteel 14
Riebeek Valley 14, *15*, 17, 18, *26*
annual events 203
location map *14*
morning market 50
Tourism Bureau 51
Riebeek-Wes 14, 18
Rietmond farm 183
rock art 184, 189, 198
see also San
Rock Art Management Plan 189
roads
Langberg 122
N7 (inland) 10, 14, 102, 150
R27 (coastal) 10, 35
R46 14
R399 102
Rocherpan Nature Reserve 98
contact number 99
rock art 10, *see also* San rock paintings
Rondeberg Nature Reserve 50
contact number 51
Rondegat River 169
rooibos (*Aspalathus linearis*) 178

S

sabre-toothed cat (fossil) 61
Salamander Bay 62
Saldanha Bay 35, 62, 72, 75
whaling station 63
Saldanha Islands 93
Saldanha Tourism (contact number) 99
salt trade 95
sandveld 133
San 157, 189
rock paintings 152, *188*, 189
Sanddrif 169
camp site 198
on Dwarsrivier farm (contact number) 199
SANParks 72
satin flower, yellow (*pietsnot*) (*Grielum humifusum*) 85
SA Young Wine Show 162
Schaafsma Chartering (contact number) 99
Schaapen Island view *59*
seals
Cape fur 195
fossils 61
seaweed 39
Seb Di Capua Charters (contact number) 99
Seb's Fishing Tackle shop 59
contact number 99
Seb's Lagoon Guide and map 59
Second Boer War 18
Seeberg viewing point *66*
Sevilla Trail 184
Sevilla and Traveller's Rest 169
Settlers 134, 157
sheep shearing 30
shoemaking 183, 187
Skydive Citrusdal (contact number) 199
skydiving, tandem 198
Smuts, Jan Christiaan 17, 18, 21
snapdragon flowers 124
Sneeuberg 167
Sneeukop 167
snoek (fish) 35, *76*
Sonquas people 17

sorrel (*suring*) (*Oxalis*) 85
sour rod (*suurlat*) *see* honey bell bush
South African Human Sciences Research Council 48
South African Museum 63
South African National Biodiversity Institute (SANBI) 136
South African National Parks 43
South African Natural Heritage Site 134, 189
southern mullet (*Liza richardsonii*) 89
Southern Right whale (*Eubalaena australis*) *63*, 63, 65
spoonbills 191
springbok 68
Stadsaal (City Hall) cave 158
'Star of Bethlehem' plant 47
Steenboksfontein farm 198
steenbras, white (fish) 89
steentjie fish 59
St Helenasfontein (historic farm) 127
St Joseph sharks 89
Stofbergsfontein 75
Stompneusbaai 99
St Peter's Church 72
strandloper ancestors 86
strandveld (beach vegetation) 91, 92
Strassberger's Hotel (contact number) 199
Strassbergers Veldshoe Factory 183, 187, 198
  contact number 199
stumpnose fish 59
sugarbirds, Cape 122
surfing 191
suring flowers *100*
Swartland (Black Land) 14, 27, 150

T

Tamarak
  Cottages (contact number) 147
  Protea Farm 122, 146
Tannie Evita, *see* Uys, Pieter-Dirk
terns, Antarctic 95
tidal mudflats 61
Tietiesbaai 78, 98
tortoise, angulate 68, 98, 138
Townshend, William 36
Tra-Tra River 183
Travellers Rest 184
  contact number 199
  Country Inn & Guest House (contact number) 51
Tretchikov, Vladimir (painting by) *49*
Trinity Guest Lodge (contact number) 51
Tsaarsbank 68

U

Uys, Pieter-Dirk (Evita Bezuidenhout) 48

V

van der Lubstadt, Frantz Joosten 30–31
van der Stel, Willem Adriaan 14, 27, 40
van Riebeeck, Jan 14
Vanrhynsdorp 187
veld
  finds 133
  food 84–85
Velddrif 10, 86, 102
  annual events 203
  bell 96
  Salt Works 95
  Tourism (contact number) 99
  Waterfront 96
veldkool/hottentotskool/bokkool (*Trachyandra falcate*) 85
velskoen factory 183, 187, 198
Venus protea 122
Verlorenvlei 93, 191
Versfeld, J. P. E. 114
Versfeld Pass 114, 146
Verwoerd, Hendrik Frensch 48
Villa Verano (contact number) 99
viltvingers (*Codium fragile*) 39
Visser, Jan (artist) 82, *83*
Vredenburg 75
vygies *108*, 124

W

waterbirds 98
waterblommetjie (*Aponogeton distachyos*) 10, 140–141, *142*
  -bredie 85, 146
watermelon, sugared *112*
water sports 98
Waylands Guest House (contact number) 51
Weskus Spens (home produce store) 84–85
West Coast
  Bird Club 93, 95
  contact numbers 99
  Fossil Park 10, *60*, 61, 98
  National Park 10, 43, 65, 68, 93, 98, 114
  seascape *99*
  Tourism 51
West Coast rock lobster (*Jasus lalandii*) 191
Western Cape Wader Study Group 61
whales 35, 62–63, 68
  blue 63
  Bryde's 63
  fossils 61
  humpback 63, 65
  Southern Right 63, 65
  terms 65
whale-watching industry 62
whaling station 35, 62–63
Wheatfields Country House (contact number) 147
white-water paddling 169
wildcat, African 68
wildebeest 68, 189
wine
  Cederberg Cellars 198
  Groote Post 40, *41*
  varietal 27
Winkel op Paternoster, Die *78*
Winkelshoek Curio Shop and Farm Stall (contact number) 147
Witteboomen farm 44
Wittewater (White Water) 106–107, 146, 183
  mission station 105
Wolfberg
  Arches 157, *158*, 169
  Cracks 198
wood-burning stoves 144
World Checklist of Monocotyledons 136
World Heritage Site 157
Wupperthal 169, 173, 183, 198
  annual events 203
  mission station 105, 183

Y

yellowtail fish 89
Yzerfontein 10, *34*, 35, 65
  annual events 203
  fish market 50
  Lighthouse (contact number) 51
  Tourism Bureau 51

Z

zebra
  Cape mountain 189
  mountain 68
Zonquasdrift 17